Stephen Curry: The Incredible Story of One of Basketball's Sharpest Shooters

An Unauthorized Biography

By: Clayton Geoffreys

Table of Contents

Foreword

In recent years, a sharpshooter has been emerging in the NBA. That sharpshooter is Stephen Curry. Since entering the league in 2009, Steph Curry has helped a once forgotten franchise rebuild to become a serious contender in the Western Conference, including an NBA championship in 2015. Beyond his team accomplishments with the Golden State Warriors, Steph has accrued a number of individual recognitions including going down in history as the all-time leader of most three-point field goals made in a single NBA season. This has all been done in his twenties. Needless to say, Steph Curry has an incredible NBA career ahead of him and will be entertaining fans for many years to come. Thank you for downloading *Stephen Curry: The Incredible Story of One of Basketball's Sharpest Shooters*. In this unauthorized biography, we will learn Steph's incredible life story and impact on the game of basketball. Hope you enjoy and if you do, please do not forget to leave a review!

Also, check out my website at claytongeoffreys.com to join my exclusive list where I let you know about my latest books and give you goodies!

Cheers,

Clayton Geoffreys

Introduction

We were all taught that children inherit the genes of their parents. Their physical appearance and sometimes even their disease history becomes part of who we are. Most of the time, we also copy their attitudes and mannerisms. In the case of Wardell "Steph" Curry, one couldn't help but wonder if he also inherited his NBA father Dell Curry's shooting touch. An NBA pundit said that great shooters are not made, they are born.

Fans of the league have been very privileged to watch some of the greatest shooters that ever played the game. From the likes of Pete Maravich, Larry Bird, former three-point record holder Reggie Miller, and the one who unseated him, Ray Allen, we have witnessed the greatest shooting displays on the planet. However, some scribes rate Steph Curry, even in the early stages of his career, as the greatest shooter in history. Although this is still debatable, some of Curry's performances have backed up this somewhat outrageous statement, especially to loyal Miller or Allen fans. On February 27, 2013, Curry lit up Madison Square Garden, scoring a career-best 54 points, including 11 of 13 from deep. He also owns the league record for three-pointers made in a single season with 272, set during the 2012-13 season, breaking Allen's record.

Despite his success nowadays, life wasn't always a bed of roses for Curry. Having an ex-NBA player for a father doesn't always automatically mean that the son is also going to become one; just ask Marcus Jordan, Michael Jordan's son, who hasn't played a single game yet in the NBA. Curry wasn't heavily recruited in high school despite his celebrated status as a son of an ex-NBA player and his numerous accomplishments. Most scouts dismissed him as being too small in stature to be successful in college basketball. He didn't allow this setback from letting him realize his dream as he went on to blossom as a player at the mid-major school Davidson, a small college close to their home in Charlotte, North Carolina.

As in the biblical story of David versus Goliath, Davidson, led by Curry, took down the "giant" college programs one by one during the 2008 NCAA Tournament. They finally fell out of steam in the Elite Eight against Kansas. This Cinderella run pushed Curry into the national spotlight, as he was at the front and center of Davidson's upset wins.

Curry went on to be chosen by the Golden State Warriors during the 2009 NBA Draft. His trials didn't stop at the NBA level, however; because of his nagging ankle injuries during his first three years, he was compared to Grant Hill, whose sky-high potential wasn't fully realized due to being constantly injured early in his career.

As he has always done, Curry bounced back and has proven his good health during the last two seasons, setting records on the way to stardom. He has led a once dormant Golden State franchise to relevance once again. With another deadly shooter, Klay Thompson, his "Splash Brother," by his side and a very deep roster headed by the likes of David Lee, Andrew Bogut, Harrison Barnes, and Andre Iguodala, the Warriors are once again poised to make a deep run at the playoffs this season. As for Curry, the future is definitely bright as long as he manages to stay away from the injuries that plagued him during his first three years in the league.

Chapter 1: Childhood and Early Life

Being the son of a former NBA shooting guard, Stephen Curry had the ideal platform on which to learn and grow into the brilliant sharpshooter that he has become. Since his young days, Stephen has always been a basketball fanatic and lover. His father, Dell Curry, speaks of how Steph was at his first basketball game when he was only two weeks old. It is obvious that Stephen learned how to play the game by watching his father Dell in action.

Born on the 14th of March 1988 in Akron, Ohio, Wardell Stephen Curry II was quick to pick up the basketball, following in the footsteps of his father. Stephen had an incredibly sporty background at home in Ohio, surrounded by two professional athletes, his parents – Dell and Sonya Curry – who gave him much of his athletic inspiration. But that household didn't stay in Ohio very long as his father's career made the family move to various parts of North America – from Ohio to Canada to North Carolina before Steph Curry eventually found himself playing college and professional basketball; just like his old man.

Athletics Runs in the Family

Dell Curry is a former NBA shooting guard, who was well-known for his great shooting eye. It all started while he was growing up in Harrisonburg, Virginia, and his coach at Fort Defiance High School helped him by providing a pretty unique practice area – a barn[i]. It was either that or he shot hoops by using a goal that was attached to a tree in his family's yard. He spent a few hours every day practicing in the barn and even set a goal of making as many as 500 shots in one practice. It paid off, as he finished his high school career as the highest scoring player in Fort Defiance history and was one of the stars showcased in the 1982 McDonald's High School All-American game.

In addition, Dell was offered a chance to play professional baseball, a sport he also enjoyed in high school. However, he passed on the opportunity after he was selected by the Texas Rangers in the 1982 Major League Baseball Draft. Dell chose to go to Virginia Tech University, where he still played baseball in the spring. But the winter months were for basketball, and that seemed to be his true calling, even if the Baltimore Orioles also drafted Dell in the 1985 MLB Draft. While he was okay in baseball with a 3.81 ERA as a pitcher during his collegiate career, he was much better suited for the game of basketball at 6-foot-4 and about 190 pounds.

Right off the bat, Dell made an impact on a Hokies team that appeared in the National Invitational Tournament in 1983 and 1984, when that event was considered second only to the NCAA National Championship Tournament. In his freshman season, Dell averaged about 14.5 points, 3.3 assists, 3 rebounds, and almost 2 steals per game and the Virginia Tech Hokies finished with a 23-11 record that included an 85-79 win over William and Mary in the first round of the 1983 NIT Tournament on March 17, 1983; Virginia Tech then fell on the road at South Carolina, 75-68, on March 21, 1983[ii].

Dell's sophomore year saw improved statistics, as he scored 19.3 points per game while also averaging 4.1 rebounds, 2.7 assists, and 2.5 steals in another season in which the Hokies lost late in the Metropolitan Athletic Conference Tournament to Memphis on March 10, 1984. Dell helped lead the Hokies to three straight wins in the 1984 NIT Tournament, including a defeat of Georgia Tech, 77-74, on March 15, 1984. That game was followed by a 68-66 win on March 18, 1984, over South Alabama and a 72-68 win over Tennessee on March 23, 1984, to earn a spot among the final four teams in the NIT that played at Madison Square Garden in New York City. After falling to the Michigan Wolverines, 78-75, in the NIT semifinals on March 26, 1984, Dell and the Hokies won the third-place game, 71-70, over Louisiana-Lafayette on March 28, 1984, to finish the season with a record of 22-13.

Consider it a bit of a boost for the Hokies as they followed that up with a 20-9 record in the 1984-85 season and won a berth in the NCAA Tournament, although they lost in the first round to the Temple Owls, 60-57, on March 14, 1985. Dell had another good season as a junior with averages of 18.2 points, 5.8 rebounds, 3.1 assists, and 2.4 steals. But it was in his senior season that Dell made a national impact on a team that finished 22-9 and won another berth in the 1986 NCAA Tournament – averaging collegiate career highs of 24.1 points, 6.8 rebounds, 3.8 assists, and 2.6 steals. Once again, the Hokies were eliminated in the first round of the national championship tournament on March 13, 1986, with a 71-62 loss to the Villanova Wildcats. Overall, Dell finished second on the all-time list at Virginia Tech with 2,389 points and claimed the school record for steals with 295. It was a career that earned him the opportunity to play in the National Basketball Association after he was selected 15th overall in the league's 1986 draft by the Utah Jazz.

His rookie year in Utah didn't give him more than about 9½ minutes in each of his 67 appearances, and he averaged about 4.9 points in that span. The Jazz decided to trade Dell to the Cleveland Cavaliers, where his average minutes increased to about 19 per game. That led to his averaging about 10 points per game for a team that barely made the NBA Playoffs with a record of 42-40; the Cavaliers fell quickly in the first round of the Eastern Conference Playoffs to the Chicago Bulls[iii].

Dell then became eligible for the NBA's expansion draft to start the 1988-89 season and was picked by the Charlotte Hornets. During his first four seasons with the Hornets, Dell had some of the best numbers of his career, including averages of 16 points and about 1.5 steals in the 1989-90 season, when he was one of the few bright spots for a Charlotte team that finished with a record of 19-

63. Dell had his first playoff experience with the Hornets after being a star off of the bench with 15.3 points per game in 80 appearances to help Charlotte to a 44-38 record and an appearance in the Eastern Conference Semifinals. The best year of his NBA career was the 1993-94 season, when he averaged 16.3 points, 3.2 rebounds, 2.7 assists, and 1.2 steals.

Dell played for Charlotte for 10 seasons before spending a season with the Milwaukee Bucks and three with the Toronto Raptors, with his averages steadily declining before he retired in 2002. After a total of 16 seasons, Dell finished with 12,670 points, 2,617 rebounds, and another 1,909 assists. Many feel his genes were passed on to his children, especially Steph – as well as his younger brother Seth. Both were commonly seen attending many of Dell's games during his career in Charlotte.

Steph's mother was a prolific volleyball player who grew up in Radford, Virginia, and made a name for herself as a basketball and volleyball star, helping Radford High School win state championships in both sports[iv]. This led to her earning a scholarship to play volleyball for Virginia Tech in 1984. She found her own success on the volleyball court, earning a spot on the All-Metropolitan League team and she led the nation in volleyball aces. During that time, she met Dell on the campus of Virginia Tech, and after he had made his NBA debut with the Charlotte Hornets, the couple got married in 1988.

A Positive Childhood

Steph Curry grew up attending a Christian Montessori school that was formed by his mother. Believe it or not, attending a school like that was a big reason that the Curry family grew very close to each other. For the next several years, the Curry siblings all went to school together with their mom, grandmother, and aunt. It was in this school that Steph first learned about independence and accountability. Sonya was also a very strict disciplinarian. Steph remembered that, on the night before his first middle school game, he purposely skipped washing the dishes. As a consequence, his mother didn't allow him to play.

Even though both parents were successful athletes, sports weren't the first priority in the Curry household. The Curry children had no doubt about the order of priorities in their life – faith, family and academics above everything else, including sports. Sonya explained that they didn't pressure their children to pursue an athletic career like other ex-athlete parents. They had observed that many children of ex-athletes thought that the only path of life was to become athletes themselves, and didn't know what else to do as a consequence. She elaborated that they only wanted their children to be "normal and grounded." Steph is very grateful to his parents and other relatives because of the way they raised him. He adds that he and his siblings were very blessed to have such great influences in their lives while growing up.

Steph recalls that although he watched a lot of his dad's games when he was young, the best games for him as a child were the ones between him and his little brother, Seth. They used to play non-stop into the night in their backyard until their mom would yell for both of them to come inside. But little did the brothers know that they would both play in front of national audiences in the near future.

Finding Early Success on the Hardwood

But before that, Curry found himself playing very well at the middle school level while the family was living in Canada. His father was playing for the Toronto Raptors between 2001 and 2002. Stephen Curry was going to Queensway Christian College in Etobicoke, Ontario, Canada, for his seventh- and eighth-grade school years and helped the Saints team find success during those two years[v].

One of his teachers recalled how the younger Curry was impressing everyone with high games of 40 and 50 points that seemed so easy for the son of the Raptors' star and helped the Saints team go undefeated in the 2001-02 season. There really wasn't a close challenger in the area after they defeated Mentor College in a tournament championship game in which they were down by 8 points with only about a minute left. The *Toronto Star* had a story about finding some of Curry's former teachers and coaches at the school who could remember that he asked them to give him the ball and so they did[vi], resulting in a flurry of three-point field goals and steals causing a 13-point swing that gave the Saints the win.

In addition to that, Curry continued to develop his game from beyond the three-point line not only in youth basketball at the middle school level, but also through a Toronto Club team in the Toronto 5-0 that competed throughout the rest of Ontario. While basketball was created in the United States and had a long history with the NBA and other iconic leagues like the American Basketball Association, Canada has provided plenty of talent of its own and Curry would see some of that in games against other players he would later meet in the NBA. In fact, the Toronto 5-0's biggest rivals were the Scarborough Blues and Curry faced off against Cory Joseph and Kelly Olynyk. However, Curry returned to the U.S. and found himself back in Charlotte, North Carolina, where his father had his best years in basketball.

Chapter 2: High School Years

Steph attended the Charlotte Christian School in Charlotte, North Carolina. He did not waste any time beginning to showcase his skills as a premier and professional-caliber basketball player. As someone who stood only about 5-feet-6 and weighted just 125 pounds at the age of 15, Curry was a freshman called up from the junior varsity team during a state tournament game against Ravenscroft back in 2003. There wasn't much to look at, literally, as the jersey could have been mistaken for a nightgown on the very young Curry. With his team losing by double digits, Curry brought the ball down the court and confidently took a step up to a three-point attempt that hit nothing but net. That's when head Coach Shonn Brown knew that the future of the Knights' basketball program and the game plan moving forward were going to revolve around Curry.

Steph received many awards including the all-state, all-conference, and team MVP (Most Valuable Player) awards. He was a three-time letter winner and accumulated a total of 1,400 points in his career for a school record, which gave him an average of about 18 points per game. Charlotte Christian won three conference championships during Curry's run with the team and that included three appearances in the North Carolina state tournament[vii].

During Curry's senior season, he made 48 percent of his field goals as the offensive star for the Knights; they finished the season 33-3 and were the state runners-up in 2006 after losing 61-53 to Greensboro Day on February 25, 2006. It was still a good run for Curry, who also had a chance to finish his high school career on the same court as his younger brother Seth for two of those seasons[viii].

Perhaps the most shocking incident that occurred after his tremendous success in high school was that he was not offered a single scholarship from a major conference school, even though he rightfully deserved one on account of his 48 percent shooting percentage from behind the arc. Most scouts and coaches from the major programs dismissed him as being "too skinny, too short" to make an impact in college basketball. Steph was only 6 feet tall and weighed 180 pounds when he was a high school senior, prompting these remarks. Due to his relative lack of strength, Steph began the release of his shot from his navel. Realizing that this was unsustainable because it can be easily blocked and is too methodical, Dell changed his son's shot, making him bring the ball above his head before releasing it. It took Steph a while before he mastered this shot. "For three weeks I couldn't shoot outside the paint," recalled Steph. "I was really that bad before I finally figured it out."

He was only rated as a three-star recruit and did not make the national top 100-150 recruits lists on sports websites such as ESPN and Rivals. One scout even gave him a very low score of 36 out of 100 in his personal evaluation. Eric Bossi was one of the national scouts from Rivals who were not impressed with Curry's high school numbers and stated that he was too short and too skinny to be able to be an effective player for any of the big collegiate programs. He was considered good enough to make open shots without many misses and not many matched his passing, ball-handling, and work ethic. The problem was that a lot of programs and college scouts couldn't really see what Curry's full potential would be if he grew a little taller, added some more weight, and had some time to mature and improve his overall basketball ability. That's a big reason that a lot of programs in the Atlantic Coast Conference wouldn't even offer a chance for Curry to walk on to fight for a roster spot.

Nonetheless, Steph entertained a number of mid-major options; in reality, he wanted to go to Virginia Tech because of his father's Hall of Fame status there, but he was not offered a scholarship by the school. The Hokies only extended an invitation to him as a walk-on and he wouldn't have any money to pay for school outside of academic scholarships. Curry would also be placed in redshirt status where he would have a year to prove he was worth bringing onto the team while preserving a year of college eligibility. It would also be a riskier play in an attempt to get on the team in the first place while losing years of eligibility. That's why Curry chose to go a different route for playing college basketball.

The schools that did offer the young Steph Curry a scholarship were the Davidson Wildcats, Virginia Commonwealth (VCU) Rams, and the Winthrop Eagles – all mid-major programs. He chose Davidson because he liked its tightly-knit community located in Davidson, North Carolina, which features a total enrollment below 2,000 students and a good education. Having said that, Steph went on to work wonders for Davidson College, which had not won a single title game since 1969. Not being offered a scholarship by his father's alma mater was depressing, but it became motivation for the young Curry; motivation that turned out to be great for the small basketball program at Davidson that was hoping to build off of their first-round loss to Minnesota as a 15-seed in the 2006 NCAA National Championship Tournament.

Chapter 3: College Years at Davidson

Steph Curry played at Davidson College for three years. In that period, he made a massive impact to propel the Wildcats to many great performances. He turned out to be their star player. Curry picked up right where he left off from his high school days and went up from there, improving drastically year after year. His numbers kept getting better and he had some moments that would be remembered for a long time.

Freshman Year

In his first year at Davidson, Curry made an immediate impact and laid the foundation for his future success. Prior to his first appearance, his head coach had famously exclaimed, "Wait 'till you see Steph Curry. He is something special." Special indeed he was, as Steph went on to average 21.5 points per game while sporting a 40 percent three-point percentage and 46 percent field goal percentage[ix].

In his first game of the season, on the road at Eastern Michigan on November 10, 2006, Curry went 5 of 12 from the field (41.7 percent) and 3 of 7 from three-point range (42.9 percent) to score 15 points while collecting 5 rebounds, 3 assists, and 3 steals in an 81-77 win. The one difficult part of the game for Curry was ball control as a point guard, since he turned the ball over 13 times to the Eastern Michigan Eagles. He cut that down the next day on the road against the Michigan Wolverines by turning the ball over just three times. But his offense really caught fans' attention in just his second appearance as a freshman in the 78-68 loss to Michigan on November 11, 2006. Curry gave a preview of the dominance that was to come in his near future with a 32-point game, along with 9 rebounds and 4 assists; he shot 48 percent from the field (12 of 25).

Davidson bounced back in the last stop on their season-opening three-game road trip at Central Connecticut State with a 91-64 win on November 12, 2006, when Curry made 3 of 5 from behind the three-point arc (60 percent) and 4 of 10 overall for 16 points to go along with 6 rebounds, 5 assists, 3 steals, and 1 block. Curry was starting to find his offensive stride in the non-conference schedule during a 100-89 win in the home opener against the University of Illinois-Chicago on November 15, 2006; he scored 27 points, shooting 11 of 19 from the field and 3 of 6 from three-point range. Curry then lost some of that momentum by turning the ball over 10 times in an 81-75 loss to the Missouri Tigers of the Southeastern Conference on November 19, 2006, a game in which he shot only 4 of 11 from the field (36.4 percent) for just 16 points, 6 assists, 4 rebounds, and 4 steals.

After Curry scored 29 points by hitting 10 of 24 from the field (nine of 20 from three-point range) in a non-Division I contest against Colby College on November 21, 2006, in a 99-69 win, he had a tough shooting game against the Duke Blue Devils on

November 25, 2006, in a 75-47 loss; he went 2 of 9 from the field overall (22.2 percent) and just 1 of 6 from behind the three-point arc (16.7 percent) for just 5 points. It was the only game in Curry's freshman season in which he scored less than 10 points. Davidson began a long winning streak that started in December and most of January after the loss to one of the nation's top programs. It started on December 1, 2006, during a 86-61 win over Elon, in which Curry scored 11 points and continued on December 4, 2006, when Curry made 40.9 percent from the field, including 4 of 9 from behind the three-point arc, to score 24 points in a 66-63 win over North Carolina-Greensboro. Curry then scored 17 points, making 50 percent from the field, to help the Wildcats defeat the Charlotte 49ers 79-51 on December 9, 2006. After nearly a week of rest, Davidson got a very convincing 116-55 win over Mount Saint Mary on December 15, 2006, with Curry making 6 of 10 from three-point range (60 percent) and 7 of 11 overall from the field for 20 points to go along with 4 rebounds.

Curry recorded his first collegiate double-double on December 18, 2006, during a 92-80 win over Chattanooga, in which he scored 30 points and collected 11 total rebounds with 6 assists and 3 steals. He made 11 of 21 overall from the field (52.4 percent) and 6 of 13 from three-point range (46.2 percent) in that game. He scored another 19 points, shooting 43.8 percent from the field in an 83-74 road win over the Ohio Bobcats on December 21, 2006, followed by a big 75-70 win over Arizona State of the Pacific-10 Conference on December 22, 2006 – any win over a team from a major conference can be a huge boost for a mid-major program like Davidson, even if Curry only scored 10 points, shooting just 4 of 8 from the field. Davidson finished their non-conference schedule with a 71-64 win at home over Western Michigan on December 30, 2006 – he scored 23 points but that number could have been a lot higher as he made just 4 of 17 from the field for 23.5 percent shooting. Curry was perfect on all 13 of his free throws to help boost his scoring total.

Davidson entered the Southern Conference schedule as one of the favorites to win the conference and possibly earn a spot in the NCAA National Championship Tournament. It started off well as the Wildcats' winning streak continued on January 6, 2007, with an 81-73 win over Charleston where Curry made 6 of 16 from the field (two of 9 from three-point range) to score 19 points to go along with just 2 rebounds; his teammate Thomas Sander led the team with 25 points and 10 rebounds after making 10 of 14 from the field. Curry scored another 15 points after making 4 of 11 from the field and 6 of 8 from the foul line as the Wildcats defeated Furman, 71-63, on January 10, 2007; once again Sander led the team with 24 points, followed by Jason Richards' 18 points. While other players were getting the most points early in the Southern Conference schedule, Curry was still doing well as a developing freshman. He scored another 16 points with 6 rebounds and 4 assists in an 83-78 win over Wofford on January 13, 2007, followed by a team-leading 17 points when he made 5 of 9 from the field (4 of 6 from three-point range) during a 79-54 win over the Citadel on January 16, 2007; Curry also collected 4 rebounds, 3 assists, and 2 steals in that game.

Curry and Davidson lost their first conference game of the schedule on January 20, 2007, when Appalachian State defeated the Wildcats at Davidson by a score of 81-74; Curry scored 15 points, but he was able to make only 1 of 11 from behind the three-point arc and just 6 of 17 overall from the field for 35.3 percent. It was the last conference loss for Davidson in a long time, and Curry had a streak of games in which he scored 20 or more points that lasted through most of February. It started with a 101-92 high-scoring affair on January 23, 2007, when Curry scored 23 points after making 7 of 14 from the field and 4 of 10 from long distance. Curry then led the team with 25 points, making 8 of 11 from the field (5 of 8 from long range) to help the Wildcats get a 79-59 win over Western Carolina. In the next game, against Elon on January 30, 2007, Curry scored another 25 points by making 9 of 17 from the field while collecting 8 rebounds in an 88-58 blowout win on the road. Curry nearly hit the 30-point mark again in a 75-65 win at home over North Carolina-Greensboro on February 3, 2007, when he scored 29 points; most of his damage came from converting 7 of 13 from behind the three-point line to help Davidson win their 20th game of the season.

The streak continued with Curry scoring 24 points, hitting 7 of 12 from the field and 6 of 6 from the foul line to help lead the Wildcats to an 87-57 win over Chattanooga on February 6, 2007. That was followed by another 24 points in a 75-63 win at Charleston on February 12, 2007. Curry's scoring continued with 25 points on making 6 of 11 from the field (5 of 8 from behind the three-point arc) in the team's 92-59 win at Western Carolina on February 17, 2007. With the rest of their regular season schedule at home, Davidson's winning also continued with an 80-73 win over Wofford on February 19, 2007, in a game where Curry hit 50 percent of his total field goals, including 4 of 9 from three-point range, to score 28 points, along with 5 rebounds. Curry then helped the Wildcats with 24 points, 6 rebounds, and 4 assists in a 75-57 win over Furman on February 22, 2007. Curry's 20 points (or more) per game scoring streak ended in the final regular-season game on February 24, 2007, with an 87-70 win over the Citadel; Curry was just 5 of 11 from the field, with 3 of 9 from three-point range, to score 18 points.

Davidson only had one mark on their Southern Conference record in the regular season with a record of 14-1 before going into the conference tournament where the winner got an automatic bid to the NCAA National Championship Tournament. In the first round against Chattanooga, Davidson got the 78-68 win on March 1, 2007, when Curry made 6 of 16 from the field (37.5 percent) and only 3 of 11 from three-point range for 20 points, with 5 rebounds, 4 assists, and 3 steals. Twenty-four hours later, on March 2, 2007, Curry had a much better game shooting from long distance at 6 of 10 (60 percent) and 9 of 14 overall from the field (64.3 percent) to lead the team with 30 points, along with 4 rebounds and 2 assists. In the Southern Conference Championship on March 3, 2007, Curry made 10 of 24 from the field (41.7 percent) and 5 of 7 on the foul line to score 29 points with 8 rebounds in a 72-65 win over Charleston. It was a thrilling game in which Curry played 40 minutes, a season-high.

The win gave Davidson a record of 29-4 and the automatic berth in the NCAA Tournament. Because of their conference, Davidson was given a 13-seed in the tournament and placed in the Midwest Regional to face the fourth-seeded Maryland Terrapins, who were given at at-large bid into the tournament after compiling a 24-8 record in the tough Atlantic Coast Conference. In the game played in Buffalo, New York, on March 15, 2007, Davidson fell in the first round against Maryland, 82-70. Curry scored 30 points, making 9 of 21 from the field (42.9 percent) and 5 of 14 from three-point range (35.7 percent), but he fouled out after playing 36 minutes. Richards was the only other player to score in double digits with 11 points. Davidson shot just 34.3 percent from the field with most of the offense coming from their star freshman. He was also an essential part of Davidson being able to earn their first NCAA Tournament bid in almost 40 years.

Even though they were eliminated in the first round of the national championship tournament, it was considered a successful season for the Davidson Wildcats with the development of their young star, Curry. The talented freshman averaged 21.5 points per game and played in all 34 of Davidson's games. He shot 46.3 percent from the field overall and 40.8 percent behind the three-point arc.

Curry surpassed the previous record for most points scored by a freshman at Davidson by scoring his 502nd point. He helped lead the Davidson Wildcats to a Southern Conference regular-season title. Curry was second only to Texas' Kevin Durant among freshman scorers. At the end of his freshman year, he had a marvelous 730 points, 366 of which came on three-pointers. Curry's success in his freshman year did not end there, as he was selected to represent USA in the FIBA Under-19 World Championship, where he excelled again. He was selected as the Southern Conference Freshman of the Year, tournament MVP, and a member of the all-tournament team, along with many other prestigious awards.

Sophomore Year

In his sophomore year, Stephen Curry had more chances to impress. It started early with a non-conference exhibition against Emory, a 120-56 blowout on November 9, 2007, when Curry made 10 of 15 from the field, with 5 of 8 coming from behind the three-point arc to score 27 points while collecting 7 rebounds and 7 assists. He was the star performer in most of Davidson's matches and stepped up to face stronger teams like North Carolina, North Carolina State, and Duke. Even though the Wildcats lost all of these games by close margins, Curry was the standout player, averaging 24.3 points in these three games along with making some spectacular assists and unselfish plays.

The first game against major conference competition was on November 14, 2007, when Davidson played North Carolina at a neutral site. Curry went 8 of 22 from the field with just 2 of 12 converted three-point field goals to score 24 points in the 72-68 loss to the Tar Heels. It may have affected Davidson would lose on the road to the Western Michigan Broncos on November 21, 2007, to start the season 1-3; Curry scored 25 points, making 9 of 16 from the field (56.3 percent) and 5 of 11 from three-point range (45.5 percent). But Davidson got a couple of wins in the week leading up to their big game against Duke at their home court; confidence going in was going to be important.

After Davidson defeated North Carolina Central 98-50 on November 24, 2007, (Curry scored 16 points), and had an early Southern Conference win over Appalachian State, 71-60, on November 24, 2007 (38 points), Curry scored 20 points, making 8 of 17 from the field (4 of 7 from behind the three-point arc) to lead Davidson in a close 79-73 loss to the Duke Blue Devils, who were undefeated at the time. It was the start of a three-game losing streak in which Davidson lost to Charlotte on the road, 75-68, on December 5, 2007, when Curry scored 32 points, making 9 of 19 from the field and 7 of 8 free throws. The Wildcats then lost to the University of California-Los Angeles (UCLA) on December 8, 2007, in a 75-63 game; Curry scored just 15 points and converted on only 3 of 10 from three-point range. Davidson got a 95-74 win over the Citadel on December 13, 2007, as Curry scored 20 points in just 26 minutes on the court. He had a very good game on December 21, 2007, against North Carolina State, scoring 29 points by making 10 of 24 from the field and 7 of 15 from three-point range, but the Wildcats fell to 4-8 with a 66-65 loss. It was a tough non-conference schedule, with two of those early season wins coming against their weaker Southern Conference foes, so the team really needed to do well in their conference schedule to build momentum toward the conference tournament because it was looking less likely that Davidson could count on having enough to earn an at-large bid to the NCAA Tournament; a problem for a number of mid-major programs.

After starting the New Year with a non-conference win over Georgia Southern, 92-67, on January 3, 2008 – Curry had a double-double with 24 points and 10 rebounds while making 8 of 19 from the field – Davidson started its conference schedule with key wins over Western Carolina on January 5, 2008, by an 86-73 score, thanks to Curry's team-leading 19 points despite making just 1 of 11 from three-point range, followed by a close 59-57 win over Elon on January 9, 2008. In that gave, Curry persevered after making just 4 of 15 from the field overall (26.7 percent) and just 2 of 6 from long distance (33.3 percent) to score only 15 points. Davidson then reached the .500 mark with an 8-8 record by defeating Wofford on the road, 85-50, on January 12, 2008, when Curry impressed with 10 of 13 from the field (76.9 percent) and 3 of 5 from three-point range (60 percent) to score 26 points in just 24 minutes of time on the court. The Wildcats advanced past the .500 mark with a 73-51 win at Furman on January 16, 2008, when Curry needed to score just 14 points to help Davidson win.

Curry had plenty of high-scoring games that made his freshman season look weak. On January 19, 2008, he made 12 of 21 from the field, including 8 of 14 from three-point range, to lead all players with 37 points in Davidson's 85-58 win over Chattanooga. Curry's offense continued in the team's 82-67 win at Western

Carolina on January 21, 2008, as he made 10 of 19 from the field (52.6 percent) and 6 of 11 in long-distance shooting (54.5 percent) to lead Davidson with 29 points, along with 7 rebounds, 5 steals, and 4 assists. After that, Curry scored another 28 points in Davidson's 87-70 win over the Citadel on the road on January 24, 2008.

That didn't mean Curry was always the leading scorer for Davidson, as there were others who were starting to step up when their star had a bad shooting night – something they didn't have in some of their non-conference games earlier in the season. Thomas Sander led the team with 21 points in the Wildcats' 70-58 win over Charleston on January 26, 2008, a game where Curry was just 5 of 14 from the field for 16 points and 6 rebounds. But Curry still established himself as one of the best scoring threats in NCAA Division I basketball, which was seen in the team's 78-65 win over Wofford, as he went 11 of 20 and 6 of 12 from three-point range to score 34 points with 5 rebounds, 5 assists, and 2 steals. After scoring 24 points in a 78-71 win at Chattanooga on February 2, 2008, Curry had an overall efficient game with 12 of 18 from the field shooting (66.7 percent) to score 36 points in a 74-64 win over Elon on February 6, 2008; Curry also collected 8 rebounds and 4 steals in that game.

One of Curry's most memorable games was when the Davidson Wildcats played against UNC-Greensboro on February 13, 2008.

Coming out of halftime with a 20-point deficit, he went off, making 41 points to ultimately defeat UNC-Greensboro, 83-78. Overall, Curry made 14 of 26 from the field, just 4 of 11 from behind the three-point line, and made all 9 free throws. He also collected 7 rebounds and 4 steals in the game. His shooting percentages continued to stay at or above 50 percent for most of the remainder of the season. After scoring 26 points with 5 assists during an 86-51 win over Furman on February 16, 2008, Curry scored another 30 points in the rematch against UNC-Greensboro at Davidson on February 19, 2008; Curry was 10 of 18 from the field with 6 of 9 three-pointers to go along with 4 assists and 3 rebounds, helping to give the Wildcats a 75-66 win.

Curry nearly had a double-double with 12 points and 8 rebounds in the 60-47 win over Winthrop on February 22, 2008, when he made only 4 of 14 from the field and teammate Jason Richards led the team with 21 points and 5 assists. He did a little better with 17 points, making just 30 percent from the field – 6 out of 20 overall and 5 of 10 from three-point range – during the team's 68-55 win at home over Appalachian State on February 27, 2008. Davidson closed out the regular season with an 89-69 win on the road at Georgia Southern on March 1, 2008, in a game in which Curry shot 76.5 percent from throughout the court – including 7 of 9 from three-point distance (77.8 percent) for a total of 35 points with 4 assists and 3 rebounds. Davidson finished the regular season with an undefeated 17-0 record in conference play and won 19 straight after starting 4-8 in late December.

As the regular-season champion, Davidson was the top-seed in the Southern Conference Tournament that started on March 8, 2008, at home against Wofford, whom the Wildcats defeated 82-49, thanks to Curry shooting 50 percent overall (seven of 14) for 19 points to go along with 3 rebounds, 1 assist, and 1 block. In the next game, on March 9, 2008, Curry did better with 10 of 17 field goals (58.8 percent) and 4 of 8 from three-point distance to lead the Wildcats with 26 points, 5 rebounds, 4 assists, and 1 steal as Davidson took an 82-52 win over UNC-Greensboro. Curry scored another 23 points, making 8 of 18 from the field (44.4 percent) as Davidson defeated Elon, 65-49, in the Southern Conference Championship on March 10, 2008. This gave the Wildcats their second consecutive berth in the NCAA Tournament after nearly four decades of not being invited to the "big dance."

After Curry led the Wildcats to a 20-0 Southern Conference record and a 26-6 regular-season record, Davidson entered the 2008 NCAA Division I men's basketball tournament as the 10th seed in the Midwest Region and were matched in the first round with the Gonzaga Bulldogs, the seventh seed that had a 25-7 recording coming out of the West Coast Conference. In the first round, held on March 21, 2008, in Raleigh, North Carolina, Davidson got its first NCAA Tournament win since 1969, an 82-76 victory. Curry was almost perfect as he made 14 of 22 from the field for a field goal percentage of about 64 percent, including 8 of 10 three-point field goals. Curry finished the upset with of 40 points, 5 steals, 3 rebounds, and 2 assists.

Next came the match between Davidson and the heavily favored Georgetown Hoyas, who were the second seed after going 27-5 in the Big East Conference. On March 23, 2008, Curry showed tremendous resilience when he brought his team back into the lead after overcoming a 17-point deficit to shockingly defeat Georgetown by 4 points, 74-70. He led the comeback effort with 30 spectacular points, 25 of which came in the second half. By the end of the game, Curry was 8 of 21 from the field and made 9 of 10 from the foul line while also collecting 5 assists, 3 rebounds, and 3 steals. Steph Curry was just getting started with the win over the Hoyas.

In the next round, he overcame the opposition's top defender, Michael Flowers, when he scored 33 points in an easy win over third-seeded Wisconsin by a score of 73-56 in the Sweet Sixteen matchup on March 28, 2008. Curry was much more effective in this game, shooting 50 percent while making 6 of 11 from behind the three-point arc; Curry also collected 4 steals, 4 assists, and 3 rebounds. This paved the way to Davidson's first Elite Eight appearance since 1969.

In the NCAA Midwest Regional Final on March 30, 2008, Curry pulled all the stops in an attempt to seal a win, but unfortunately Davidson fell against the Kansas Jayhawks in a low-scoring thriller that the Wildcats lost by an agonizing 2 points on March 30, 2008. Curry took a large number of shots while only going 9 for 25 from the field (36 percent) and 4 of 16 from three-point range (25 percent) to score a total of 25 points to go along with 4 rebounds, 3 assists, and 1 steal. Curry made a three-point field goal with 54 seconds left in the game before calling a timeout. The team was able to secure the final shot with eight seconds left, but Richards missed from long distance as time expired for the game and Davidson's "Cinderella" season.

Curry's numbers had skyrocketed once again as he increased his points per game and led the Southern Division with 25.9 points, 4.6 rebounds, and 2.9 assists per game. He made 162 three-point shots, setting a new record, along with a massive 931 points. He also increased his statistics in all other areas of his game to become a very well-rounded basketball player. His main awards for his sophomore year included the Most Outstanding Player of the Midwest Region in the NCAA Division I. This was a special award for him and was the first time since 1994 that a player from a team that had not made it to the Final Four received the award. He was also nominated in the Breakthrough Player of the Year category.

Sophomore year was when Stephen Curry began to cement his name in the history books with many significant milestones. With that, he still had not yet finished his career with the Wildcats of Davidson College.

Junior Year

Following his great success in 2008, Curry was prepared to take on the big leagues: the NBA. However, he announced that he would play one last season for Davidson prior to his run for a spot in the NBA. At that time, players had to be one year removed from high school graduation before they were able to eligible for the NBA's annual rookie draft. But Curry was one of the rare college stars who played beyond their impressive freshman seasons.

Curry wasted no time preparing for the NBA, starting on November 14, 2008, during a 107-83 win over Guilford; he had a double-double, scoring 29 points and collecting 10 assists, shooting 9 of 20 from the field (45 percent) and 9 of 10 from the foul line. Curry almost had a rare triple-double, adding 9 steals to his stat line. Three days later, on November 17, 2008, Curry converted on 14 of 19 field goals for 73.7 percent, with 4 of 6 three-point shots made, to score 33 points in another near double-double with 9 assists and 4 steals during a 99-64 win over James Madison.

In an 82-78 loss to the Oklahoma Sooners on November 18, 2008, he scored a career-high 44 points by making 12 of 29 field goals (41.4 percent), including 6 of his 15 attempts behind the three-point arc (40 percent) and all 14 of his free throws. He kept up this high-scoring streak and led the Wildcats to many victories. One of these was against Winthrop on November 21, 2008, in which he dished out another career high of 13 assists during a 97-70 win; Curry also hit 8 of 16 field goals (50 percent), including 5 of 12 from three-point distance (41.7 percent), to score 30 points, along with those 13 assists and 3 steals in another double-double. Curry almost hit the 40-point mark again on November 24, 2008, during a 76-60 win over Florida Atlantic. Against the Owls, Curry made 13 of 21 from the field for 61.9 percent while hitting 5 of 9 three-pointers (55.6 percent) for 39 points, 4 rebounds, 4 assists, and 1 block.

Unfortunately for Curry on November 25, 2008, he had the worst game of his collegiate basketball career with zero points in 32 minutes of playing time during the Wildcats' 78-48 win over Loyola (Maryland); he took only 3 shots from the field and didn't get a chance to shoot from the foul line. But that lack of performance didn't last long as he continued on a pace for a record-breaking season. He picked up business by matching his highest single-game score again in another game with North Carolina State on December 6, 2008, a home win by the score of

72-67. Against the Wolfpack, Curry went 15 of 33 from the field and 10 of 13 on the foul line to finish with 44 points to go with 3 steals, 3 assists, and 2 rebounds. The Davidson Wildcats earned a second straight win over a major conference opponent with a 68-65 victory at West Virginia on December 9, 2008, despite Curry making only 9 of 27 for 33.3 percent from the field. He did tally another double-double with 27 points and 10 assists while also collecting 4 rebounds, 4 steals, and 2 blocks.

But Curry was making himself known as one of the nation's best scorers as he showed in a 100-95 victory at home over Chattanooga on December 13, 2008; he converted on 11 of 22 field goals (50 percent), with 5 of 11 from three-point range (45.5 percent) and 14 of 18 from the foul line to finish with 41 points, along with 6 assists and 4 rebounds. Granted, Curry wasn't always going to score 40 points as seen in Davidson's 76-58 loss at Purdue on December 20, 2008, when he shot just 19.2 percent from the field and just 2 of 12 from three-point range for 13 points – but he did almost have a double-double with 8 rebounds and 6 assists.

After the tough scoring night against the Boilermakers, Curry did much better in the final game of December and the first week of January. During a conference game at Charleston on December 29, 2008, Curry made 11 of 25 field goals (44 percent) to finish with 29 points, 9 rebounds, 7 rebounds, and 3 steals in a 79-75 win.

Less than a week later, on January 3, 2009, at home against Samford, Curry didn't have to take a lot of shots as he made 7 of 14 from the field overall – most of his attempts were from long range as he was near perfect with 5 of 6 three-point field goals – to score 21 points with 8 assists, 4 rebounds, 4 steals, and 1 block during a 76-55 win. But in some games when Curry played well, the team overall could not defeat some of the top teams in the country, as happened in the previous games against Oklahoma and Purdue. Davidson was unable to get over this hump on January 7, 2009, while visiting the Duke Blue Devils in a 79-67 loss where Curry was effective with 29 points, 8 rebounds, and 6 assists, making 10 of 22 from the field, although he was unable to hit the mark often from three-point range, with just 1 out of 8 made.

With their focus now primarily on the Southern Conference, Davidson then traveled to the Citadel for an 84-69 win on January 10, 2009, when Curry made 50 percent from the field (half of those field goals were from behind the three-point line with 4 of 8 converted) and sank 12 of 14 free throws to lead the team with 32 points, along with 6 rebounds, 5 assists, and 5 steals. A few days later, on January 14, 2009, Curry made 11 of 18 from the field (61.1 percent), 6 of 10 from three-point range (60 percent) and 11 of 12 from the foul line to score 39 points in an 83-68 win over Elon. The Wildcats were in the middle of a 10-game winning streak after that tough loss to Duke and Curry was often scoring 30 or more points to help Davidson look as strong as they had the last two seasons. During the team's 83-43 win over Furman on January 21, 2009, Davidson made 12 of 18 from the field for 66.7 percent, with 6 of 10 from behind the three-point arc for 30 points, 5 assists, and 5 steals.

There were a number of games in which Curry was close to double-doubles and triple-doubles, including Davidson's 79-56 win over Wofford on January 24, 2009, (33 points, 7 rebounds, and 7 assists) and a 92-70 win at Chattanooga on January 28, 2009 (32 points, 8 assists, and 5 rebounds). On February 2, 2009, Curry had a near triple-double with 26 points, 8 rebounds, and 8 assists during an 89-65 win at home over Western Carolina. That was followed by his scoring 29 points and collecting 8 rebounds during Davidson's 75-54 win on the road over UNC-Greensboro on February 5, 2009. Davidson's 10-game winning streak ended February 7, 2009, with a 77-75 loss to Charleston, in which Curry struggled from the field by shooting 7 of 23 (30.4 percent) for 25 points. But he rebounded quickly in the next game at Wofford on February 12, 2009, when he made 14 of 24 field goals (58.3 percent) with 5 of 8 from three-point range for 39 points to help Davidson earn the 78-61 win.

Curry continued to be the focal point of Davidson's offense as he earned another double-double with 20 points and 10 rebounds during a 70-49 win over UNC-Greensboro on February 25, 2009.

As he continued his junior season, Curry found enormous success. He reached many incredible milestones in a very short period. He surpassed the 2,000-point mark in just 83 games. He also became Davidson College's second-leading scorer in history shortly after that. He did not stop there, as a 34-point game against Georgia Southern during a 99-56 win on February 28, 2009, pushed him ahead of John Gerdy, making him the Wildcats' highest scorer ever. The regular season was concluded with a 90-78 win on the road at Elon on March 2, 2009, when Curry scored 26 points by making 8 of 16 from the field and 8 of 10 on the foul line; Curry also collected 5 assists, 4 steals, and 3 rebounds in that game.

Under Stephen Curry's leadership, Davidson lost a mere 2 games and won 18 in conference play. Despite their impressive conference record and the lobbying of their coach and even coaches of other programs, Davidson failed to get a slot in the NCAA Tournament this time around. In the Southern Conference Tournament, Curry scored 43 points in the quarterfinals during an 84-68 win over Appalachian State on March 7, 2009. It was the third highest ever scored in the conference tournament thanks to Curry making 11 of 18 from the field (61.1 percent), 5 of 10 behind the three-point arc and converting on 16 of 18 from the foul line. But on March 8, 2009, Davidson lost in the Southern Conference semifinals by a score of 59-52 to Charleston; Curry struggled from long distance, making only 2 of 11 three-point field goals and 5 of 18 from the field overall (27.8 percent) for just 20 points.

At the end of the season, Curry was the leading scorer in the country, but was not among the stars showcased in the NCAA National Championship Tournament. Davidson managed to secure a slot in the 2009 National Invitational Tournament – also known as the NIT – where they were the sixth seed. In the first round of the NIT on March 17, 2009, Curry made 9 of 19 field goals (47.4 percent), with 5 of 9 coming from the three-point distance to finish with 32 points; despite turning the ball over 7 times, Davidson got the 70-63 win on the road at South Carolina.

Curry followed that performance with 26 points in the semifinals game at Saint Mary's on March 23, 2009, converting 11 of 27 from the field (40.7 percent) and 4 of 10 from three-point range, along with 9 rebounds, 5 assists, and 2 steals. But Davidson lost that game. Curry concluded his college career with his best numbers yet, sporting an average of 28.6 points per game. Curry also was named as NCAA All-American first-team player.

Stephen Curry chose to leave Davidson after his junior year. In his 104 total games at Davidson, Curry averaged 25.3 points, 4.5 rebounds, and 5.7 assists per game. His 2,635 total points and 414 total three-pointers are both Davidson records. That was a smart move for him, since he was already one of the best players in college basketball. He was all set to move on to the NBA.

In his college career, Curry had many highs and lows. He even went scoreless in a game, but this was due to the opposing coach assigning two defenders to him at all times. As a result, his teammates were often left with wide open shots, and they still won that game. In the end, Curry left Davidson as one of the best players, if not the very best, that the Wildcats had ever seen. He soon joined the NBA as a first-round, seventh overall pick of the Golden State Warriors.

Chapter 4: Stephen's NBA Career

Curry made the right choice when he decided to claim eligibility for the 2009 NBA Draft. He had reached the peak of college basketball and probably went down in history as Davidson's best basketball player ever. With numbers like his and experience from playing on the US U19 team, with whom Curry won a silver medal in 2007, he had boosted his chances of being selected as a top 10 draft pick. He also managed to break some impressive records in his junior year of college, including the all-time scoring record for Davidson and the Southern Conference, school career records for free throws, three-pointers, 30-point games, 40-point games, and the single-season NCAA record for three-point field goals. Needless to say, Steph Curry had a storied college career. Everything looked good for a kid whose only goal when he first started playing basketball was to be taller than Muggsy Bogues, his dad's teammate from his Charlotte days. No worries there, since Bogues only stood at 5-foot-3.

2009 NBA Draft

In a draft class that was considered to be one of the weakest since 2000, when Kenyon Martin was selected with the top pick, Curry was selected seventh overall by the Golden State Warriors. Nevertheless, the class had a handful of potential all-star players, like Blake Griffin, James Harden, Ricky Rubio, and, of course,

Steph Curry. Blake Griffin was the odds-on favorite to be the first overall pick in the whole draft and the Clippers did not hesitate. The Los Angeles Clippers took the best big man coming out of Oklahoma University, who was available with the first overall pick. Almost every team that was a part of the lottery desperately needed a point guard or shooting guard on their squad.

Minnesota held the best position as they had two consecutive picks in the top 5. Before the Timberwolves had their consecutive turns, the Memphis Grizzlies gambled and picked Hasheem Thabeet out of the University of Connecticut, which later became a pure Darko Milicic case. Oklahoma City needed a shooter who would transform the Westbrook-Durant tandem into a trio, but they picked James Harden out of Arizona State before Curry and Rubio. The Kings surprised everybody when they selected Tyreke Evans out of Memphis University; Sacramento made that selection because they desperately needed a true point guard. It was an element that they had been missing since the Mike Bibby era during the late 1990s and early 2000s.

So the Minnesota Timberwolves had the chance to create one of the most compelling potential combination of a point guard and shooting guard in recent NBA history. They could pick Rubio and Curry with their two consecutive picks, but they opted against it. They went ahead with Rubio, but instead of Curry they chose Syracuse guard Jonny Flynn. One of the reasons why the

Timberwolves avoided drafting Curry was because he refused to train with the team before the draft and said that he would not be willing to play for a team that did not have a coach; Kevin McHale had a questionable status at the time. If Minnesota had made the right decision then and in the next draft, they could have ended up with a starting five that included DeMarcus Cousins (they picked Wesley Johnson in 2010 instead), Kevin Love, Curry, and Rubio. Sounds intimidating, doesn't it? But that's not how things went, nor did the Timberwolves even really know what they passed on.

At this point in the draft, New York Knicks head Coach Mike D'Antoni was rubbing his hands with excitement while his team was sitting at the eighth overall position in the draft order. It was said that D'Antoni was impressed with Curry's performance in the two pre-draft exhibition games against the Knicks. At the time, New York had traded their starting guard Quentin Richardson to the Memphis Grizzlies, and they lacked a prolific shooter after getting rid of Jamal Crawford and ending the Marbury drama at the beginning of the year. Keeping all of this in mind, Curry would have become an instant starter on the team and a possible leader for the confused squad. It was a good scenario, but the Golden State Warriors made a decision that nobody expected. By selecting Curry with the seventh overall selection in the 2009 NBA Draft, the Warriors added him to a roster filled with undersized shooting guards, led by Jamal Crawford and Monta Ellis. The Warriors were excited that Curry fell to the seventh pick because the draft scouts were promoting how great a pure shooter he was while at Davidson College; he was credited with being able to shoot effectively and efficiently while off balance as an overall prolific scoring threat who could be just as dangerous off the dribble as he was when holding the ball at the top of the key. Obviously, Curry was also known for having quite a decent range on his shot, which was best seen when he was shooting from behind the three-point arc at the collegiate level. Curry was also applauded for knowing how to move the ball in an effort to juke away and lose a defender in addition to having good vision who was able to rebound while being undersized against most who play near the rim.

Crawford was traded to the Atlanta Hawks on draft day for Acie Law and Speedy Claxton. It was crystal clear even back then that the Warriors were clearing up some needed space for their future star guard. General Manager of the Phoenix Suns, Steve Kerr, stated in an interview years later that, at one point, the Phoenix Suns and the Golden State Warriors were in talks of a trade that involved Amar'e Stoudemire and Steph Curry. Amar'e would have been sent to Golden State and Steph would have been traded on draft night to Phoenix. Fortunately for Golden State, the deal never reached NBA front offices because of Stoudemire's health issues at the time. Larry Riley, then general manager of the Golden State franchise, can thank God for Stoudemire's health issues at the end of June 2009, because had the trade gone through, Golden State would not be in the position they are in today.

Rookie Season[x]

The Golden State Warriors did not waste time once Steph Curry was drafted. They signed Curry to a four-year contract on July 8, 2009. The deal was estimated to be worth $13 million, which was slightly above the NBA rookie pay scale for that season. Golden State needed the help because they had one of their weakest rosters in recent years and this proved to be an excellent opportunity for Curry to showcase his skills.

Curry did not disappoint, as he started his NBA campaign with great authority. He scored 14 points by converting 7 of 12 from the field, dished out 7 assists and had 4 steals in his first appearance as a Warrior in a one-point loss, 108-107, to Houston on October 28, 2009. Much of the first two months of the season was spent adjusting to the NBA schedule. In most of Curry's college seasons, the Davidson Wildcats played 34 games at the most between late October and early April, while the NBA season is about six months long and comprises 82 games in the regular season. While he was starting, he wasn't getting a large bulk of the offensive opportunities, and there were a number of games in which Curry scored in single digits. But, for the most part, he was scoring between 10 and 19 points for the months of November before he got his first game with 20 or more points on December 7, 2009, in a 104-88 loss on the road to the Oklahoma City Thunder; Curry made 9 of 14 from the field (64.3 percent), including 2 of 4 from behind the three-point arc for a total of 22 points, with 4 rebounds, 4 steals, and 2 assists. But the Warriors were still led by the veteran Monta Ellis, who led the team with 31 points on 12 of 28 from the field (42.9 percent) and 6 of 8 from the foul line.

Regardless, Curry still had a couple of flashes in that period, such as 27 points and 8 rebounds on 9 of 17 from the field (52.9 percent) – which also included making 5 of 9 from long range (55.6 percent) – while collecting 8 rebounds, 4 assists, and 3 steals during a 118-109 loss at home against the Washington Wizards on December 18, 2009. Less than a week later, on December 23, 2009, Curry recorded his first double-double in the NBA, scoring 17 points and collecting 10 rebounds despite the team losing to the New Orleans Hornets, 108-102. Another great performance from Curry was on January 5, 2010, against the Denver Nuggets when he recorded 26 points, 5 rebounds, 6 assists, and 3 steals in a tight loss, 123-122.

Shortly after this, Monta Ellis suffered a minor injury, which gave Curry more freedom and more offensive opportunities. He embraced the role of a floor general in the absence of Ellis and had two terrific games between January 23 and February 10, 2010. He set a career high in points when he scored 32 against the New

Jersey Nets on January 22, 2010, during a 111-79 win. Curry was efficient, making 11 of 21 field goals while also converting on 7 of 8 free throws. Curry also collected 7 assists and 4 steals. But he topped that career-high score on February 10, 2010, during the Warriors' 132-102 win over the Los Angeles Clippers, a game in which Curry produced his first triple-double with 36 points, 13 assists, and 10 rebounds (including 7 of 11 three-point shooting). During the 11-game span starting and ending with those games, Curry averaged 21.7 points while shooting 46 percent from the field and 43.1 percent from three-point range.

With how well he had played as a rookie, Curry was a part of the 2009 All-Star event, participating in the three-point shootout held February 13, 2010, at American Airlines Center in Dallas, Texas[xi]. The rest of the field featured a number of good long-range shooters like Chauncey Billups (Detroit Pistons) and Channing Frye (Phoenix Suns). The scoring was simple, with each of the five stations having four total basketballs – three regular for 1 point and one "money ball" that was worth 2 points to provide a maximum score of 25 points. Curry had the best first-round score with 18 points and earned a spot in the final round. But Boston Celtics forward Paul Pierce scored 20 points in the finals while Curry had just 17 points for second place; followed by Billups in third with 14 points.

Curry also participated in the annual NBA Rookie Challenge, in which the NBA top rookies competed against second-year players in a special exhibition[xii]. Curry joined a roster that featured other first-round selections like Oklahoma City's James Harden, Milwaukee's Brandon Jennings, and Sacramento's Tyreke Evans. As the rookies defeated the sophomores 140-128 on February 12, 2010, in Dallas, Curry scored 14 points to help his team win, making 6 of 11 from the field while also collecting 2 assists and 1 rebound in about 22 minutes on the court.

During the season, he became part of an elite group of players, including LeBron James and Dwyane Wade, with five or more 30-point, 5-assist games. During Don Nelson's record-breaking 1,333[rd] win against the Minnesota Timberwolves, Curry scored 27 points and had 14 assists, 8 rebounds, and 7 steals on April 7, 2010. Many NBA analysts regarded this game as the best rookie performance of that year. Curry continued to develop as one of the league's best offensive threats, culminating in the regular-season finale on April 14, 2010, a 122-116 win on the road against the Portland Trail Blazers. He made 13 out of 25 from the field (52 percent) – with 4 of 6 from long distance (66.7 percent) – and a perfect 12 for 12 on the foul line for a new career high with 42 points; Curry also collected 9 rebounds and 8 assists to come very close to a triple-double.

After Blake Griffin did not play in the 2009-10 NBA season due to injuries, Steph Curry became a fan favorite for the Rookie of the Year (ROY) award. His only competitor was Tyreke Evans, mainly because of his ridiculous stats (Tyreke became one of only three other NBA players in history that averaged at least 20 points, 5 rebounds, and 5 assists). It was tough competing against such a stat line. Curry, on the other hand, finished the season with 17.5 points, 5.9 assists, 4.5 rebounds, and 2 steals per game. That was enough to finish second in the ROY voting and to be a part of the All-Rookie First Team. He led all first-year players in assists, steals, and three-pointers made. However, Golden State struggled to a final regular-season record of 26-56 under head Coach Don Nelson, which prompted the team's front office staff to make a change by letting Nelson go and bringing in Keith Smart for the start of the 2010-11 NBA season.

Curry's performance in his rookie season did not go unnoticed in NBA circles. Shortly after the end of the 2009-10 NBA regular season, he was selected for the U.S. National basketball team. This came as a great comfort after failing to qualify for the playoffs with the Warriors and not winning the Rookie of the Year award. Curry served as a backup guard for NBA All-Stars Kobe Bryant, Chauncey Billups, Russell Westbrook, and Derrick Rose. He averaged 4.6 points in 9 games, with his best game coming against Tunisia, where he scored 13 points on 62 percent shooting.

It is interesting that Coach Mike Krzyzewski was one of the first to reject Steph Curry in his search for a college scholarship. The Duke staff had at that time stated that the 18-year-old Charlotte Christian graduate was too skinny and too short and labeled him as a one-dimensional player. It was a noble thing for Coach K to later on admit his mistake and misevaluation of Steph Curry. After Team USA won the gold medal, Krzyzewski stated in an interview that Curry possesses a "cerebral game," not only being able to make shots, but also being able to make plays as well. But there's more about Curry's international experience later in another chapter.

Sophomore Season[xiii]

Steph Curry continued to improve in his second NBA season. While he was on the World Cup campaign with the national team, it became more and more obvious that Golden State was trying to build around him. The first step toward this was to surround him with better and bigger men to create a presence in the paint. David Lee was apparently the first choice on the Warriors' wish list. The versatile power forward was acquired in a sign-and-trade deal that sent Anthony Randolph, Kelenna Azubuike, and Ronny Turiaf to New York. Other notable signings included Dorell Wright and Lou Amundson.

Curry picked up right where he left off during the Warriors' regular-season home opener on October 27, 2010, during a 132-128 win over the Houston Rockets; he made 9 of 16 field goals (56.3 percent), with 3 of 6 from three-point range, while recording a double-double with 25 points and 11 assists. It was Monta Ellis leading the team with 46 points, making 75 percent of his 24 field goal attempts and 9 of 12 from the foul line. A little more than a week later, on November 8, 2010, Curry led the team with 34 points by making 12 of 21 from the field (57.1 percent) and all 8 free throws during a 109-102 win over the Toronto Raptors. This performance was quickly followed by his 25 points, 8 assists, and 6 rebounds during a 122-117 win visiting the New York Knicks on November 10, 2010. But no matter how well Curry played, Ellis was still leading the team with most of the offensive opportunities. For example, Ellis went 17 of 30 from the field for 40 points while Curry went 9 of 21 for 29 points with 8 assists and 5 rebounds as the Warriors lost to the Knicks at home, 125-119, on November 19, 2010.

But the second-year player out of Davidson was still going to get his big games with the Golden State Warriors. On November 30, 2010, Curry led the team with 32 points, converting on 59.1 percent from the field to go along with 5 assists, 1 steal, and 1 block while Golden State lost at home to the San Antonio Spurs 118-98. In the first game of December 2010, the Warriors fell to the Oklahoma City Thunder by a score of 114-109 on December 5, 2010, despite Curry making 14 of 20 from the field (70 percent) while scoring 39 points.

Curry led the team in assists per game and managed to start in 74 games. The most he had in a single game was 13 assists, along with scoring 23 points after shooting 10 of 18 (55.6 percent) from the field on February 13, 2011, during a 100-94 win over the Thunder; followed by Curry collecting 12 assists during Golden State's 103-93 loss at Atlanta on December 29, 2010. The one thing about Curry's statistics that season was that he was not really getting a lot of rebounds; he nearly hit double digits a few times in games that would have given him additional double-doubles and maybe a few more triple-doubles, as he had in his rookie season. The most rebounds Curry had was 11 against the Minnesota Timberwolves in a 126-123 loss on February 27, 2011; Curry also scored 33 points, converting on 13 of 21 from the field (61.9 percent) and 5 of 7 from three-point range (71.4 percent).

On a side note, Curry was also establishing himself as a great defensive player to go along with how great of a scoring threat he was becoming. During the Warriors' 120-90 loss on the road to the Chicago Bulls on November 11, 2010, Curry had a season-high 5 steals against Derrick Rose and others. There were four additional games where Curry had 4 steals, including a 110-103 win on the road against the New Orleans Hornets on January 5, 2011, and again on January 21, 2011, during a 119-112 win over the Sacramento Kings on January 21, 2011. But Curry was still getting the job done on the other end of the court, as he made 12 of 21 from the field (57.1 percent) to score 34 points to go along with 12 rebounds.

After playing in 80 games during his rookie season, Curry missed eight games due to an ankle injury, which was the first sign of upcoming problems. He had a solid season and played top-level basketball on a nightly basis with only a couple of bad games. However, he still lacked maturity and was overshadowed by his more experienced teammate, Monta Ellis, who led the team in scoring and minutes played. It became noticeable that the Warriors could not function with Ellis and Curry on the same team if they wanted to make the playoffs anytime soon. This observation was the precursor for one of them being traded from the team later on.

The one thing you could say about Curry is that he was the definition of a competitor, as noticed during his sophomore season. Perhaps his favorite player to compete with in today's game is Oklahoma City's Russell Westbrook. Curry averaged 32 points, 8 assists, and 2 steals during three meetings with the Thunder in his second season. He also beat Westbrook in the Taco Bell Skills Challenge during All-Star Weekend hosted at the Staples Center in Los Angeles. Unfortunately, the Warriors yet again failed to qualify for the playoffs despite a much better win-loss record after winning 36 games and losing 46; much better than the 26-56 record during Curry's rookie season. The 10-win increase also moved the Golden State Warriors from fourth to third place in the NBA Western Conference's Pacific Division. Unfortunately for head Coach Keith Smart, his tenure with the Warriors ended after one season, despite having improved the Golden State Warriors' performance.

Curry ended the season with an average of 18.6 points, 3.9 rebounds, 5.8 assists, 1.5 steals, and a 44.2 percent clip from three-point range. He also set a new single-season Warriors record for free throw percentage, previously held by Rick Barry from the 1977-78 season, hitting 212 of 227 free throws (93.4 percent). In addition to the Skills Challenge, he also won the NBA Sportsmanship Award for ethical conduct on the court and his activities in the community. This surely meant a lot for Curry, who is a dedicated Christian and always tries to help his fellow citizens in need.

Injury-Plagued Third Year in NBA[xiv]

At the end of the 2010-11 season, Steph Curry underwent surgery to repair torn ligaments in his right ankle, which resulted from multiple sprains during his first two seasons in the NBA. Meanwhile, the team tried to create a better roster that was led by new coach and former NBA star point guard Mark Jackson. They also tried to sign DeAndre Jordan in free agency, but the Los Angeles Clippers matched their $43 million offer sheet to the then-restricted free agent.

Because Golden State was looking to build around their young star in Curry, the Warriors struck gold on draft day with the 11th pick when they selected Washington State University's Klay Thompson, a son of former Laker player Mychal Thompson. Nobody could have predicted back then that Thompson and Curry would become perhaps the deadliest one-two combination in the NBA.

Although it didn't seem like that by the 23-43 finish to the 2011-12 NBA season, which was shortened by a lockout at the beginning of the season. That meant the NBA team played only 66 games, but the schedule was condensed, and they often played two or three games on consecutive days. When you consider that the teams also had much shorter training camps to get ready, one could be understanding when Curry scored just 4 points during the team's 105-86 loss at home to the Los Angeles Clippers on December 25, 2011.

But on the very next day on December 26, 2011, Curry bounced back with 21 points, making 7 of 12 from the field and 6 of 7 free throws during a 99-91 win over the Chicago Bulls; he also had 10 assists to record a double-double. Curry matched those 21 points on December 31, 2011, at home against the Philadelphia 76ers. But because the only other player to score in double digits was David Lee with 19 points, Philadelphia won the game in a 107-79 blowout decision. There was a chance that Klay Thompson was going to see more time on the basketball court and have a chance to show how well he could work with Curry for a potential future duo that Golden State could build around. However, the birth of this killer tandem needed to wait for a little while longer because Curry managed to appear in only 26 out of 66 games in the lockout-shortened season, due to a number of ankle problems. Curry sprained his ankle multiple times during the season, first on January 4, 2012, after he scored 20 points with 8 assists by making 7 of 11 from the field in a 101-95 loss on the road against the San Antonio Spurs. Curry tried not to miss too much time as he made his return less than three weeks later, on January 20, 2012, while the Warriors hosted the Indiana Pacers in a 94-91 loss at home, in which Curry made just 5 of 15 from the field (33.3 percent) for 12 points.

It only took a few days before Curry started to show signs that he was returning to the pre-injury form. On January 25, 2012, at home against the Portland Trail Blazers, Curry led the team with 32 points, 7 assists, 6 rebounds, and 4 steals in less than 38 minutes of playing time to help Golden State earn the 101-93 win. About a week later, on February 2, 2012, Curry earned a double-double, making 10 of 14 field goals (71.4 percent) and 7 of 8 free throws for 29 points with 12 assists, 5 rebounds, and 3 steals in the Warriors' 119-101 win over the Utah Jazz. Later on in the season, Curry converted 13 out of 17 field goals (76.5 percent), including 6 of 9 from behind the three-point arc (66.7 percent) for a season-high 36 points to go along with 7 rebounds and 7 assists during the Golden State Warriors' 109-101 win on the road against the Denver Nuggets on February 9, 2012. Nine days later, on February 18, 2012, came one of the rare games in which Curry and Ellis looked dominant with the younger star scoring 36 points after making 13 of 21 from the field (61.9 percent) and 6 of 9 from three-point range to tie that season-high mark of 36 points while collecting 6 assists. Ellis himself scored 33 points by making 45.5 percent of his 22 total field goal attempts and going 9 of 12 from the foul line, but the Memphis Grizzlies got the 104-103 win despite Curry and Ellis teaming up to score 69 points.

However, Curry once again suffered a mild foot sprain during the Warriors' 106-104 win over the Phoenix Suns, in which he scored 9 points on just 3 of 7 shooting from the field with the injury occurring after he had played only 10 minutes on February 22, 2012. After missing a few games, Curry tried to return in time to play the Atlanta Hawks on February 29, 2012; but he only lasted a few seconds before suffering another ankle injury, and he had to leave the game a lot earlier than he wanted. He tried to play a few minutes coming off the bench during a road game on March 5,

2012, when Golden State earned a 120-100 win over the Washington Wizards – Curry played a little more than nine minutes and was effective, making 5 of 7 from the field for 12 points. Curry saw an increase in minutes as a reserve on March 7, 2012, against the Memphis Grizzlies at home. While the Warriors fell 110-92, Curry played about 24 minutes and made 7 of 11 field goals to finish with 15 points, 4 rebounds, and 3 assists. Things were starting to look as if they were turning around for the better in terms of Curry's health.

But on March 10, 2012, Curry started and played about 16 minutes before he suffered another foot sprain after making 4 of 7 from the field for 10 points; Golden State was able to hold off the visiting Dallas Mavericks, 111-87. Despite leaving the game early, Curry wanted to try and play the very next night on March 11, 2012, but he played only nine minutes in one of his statistically worst games in his young NBA career, as he missed all 3 field goal attempts while collecting 3 rebounds and 1 assist during Golden State's 97-93 win over the Los Angeles Clippers.

While Curry spent the remainder of the 2011-12 season recovering from ankle injuries and undergoing season-ending surgery, newly appointed general manager Bob Myers remained active in the front office to continue sculpting the Warriors around Curry. His first move came shortly after Curry was considered medically out for the rest of the 2011-12 season and Myers was successful in getting rid of Monta Ellis to make room for Curry's comeback next season while acquiring a strong big man. This move showed the faith of the front office faith in Curry, even though he had been injury-prone the previous seasons. Myers recognized that potential in a former number one pick from Australia, Andrew Bogut. The trade that sent Bogut to the Warriors included three teams and also saw Stephen Jackson going to the Spurs, Monta Ellis signing with the Bucks and Richard Jefferson coming to the Warriors. This was only a prelude to what followed in the next two seasons as the Warriors developed into a playoff-contending franchise.

One thing that didn't remain constant was that the Golden State Warriors kept the head coach for longer than one season. Mark Jackson didn't really receive a good hand at the poker table – shortened season after NBA lockout, not a whole lot of time to prepare players during the preseason training camp, and one has to give the head coach some benefit of the double because of Curry having multiple foot and ankle injuries that kept him from being able to enter the season at 100 percent health. The Warriors may not have known this when they decided to keep Jackson, but they were about to give a second chance to a coach who was going to change the culture from struggling California team into a winning culture that competed for spots in the NBA Playoffs. It was hard to believe at the time, considering how tough the Golden State Warriors had fought just to try to get as close to the .500 win-loss mark and found themselves not having made the playoffs since the 2006-07 season, when Nelson's Warriors were 42-40 for third place in the NBA Pacific Division and earned a first-round upset over the Dallas Mavericks before losing in the Western Conference Semifinals to the Utah Jazz. The Warriors did have a 48-34 record in the 2007-08 season, but Golden State was only able to earn a spot as the ninth best team in the very competitive Western Conference.

Rise to Stardom[xv]

After a disappointing 2011-12 NBA season and yet another failed attempt by the Warriors to qualify for the playoffs, Steph Curry was back for the following season. The Golden State front office made some key moves during the offseason and this Warrior squad looked as good as the one that had eliminated the top-seeded Dallas Mavericks back in 2007 in the first round of the playoffs, the Warriors' last playoff appearance. Curry had the necessary help under the basket from two big men in David Lee and Andrew Bogut. He also paired up with Klay Thompson in the backcourt, who had had a promising rookie campaign, averaging 12.5 points, 2.4 rebounds, and 2.0 assists while playing about 24 minutes per game and converting on 44.3 percent from the field overall. The Warriors also drafted Harrison Barnes, a highly touted 20-year-old athletic forward, who joined the team as a rookie and was expected to take over the starting role at small forward after playing for the

North Carolina Tar Heels. To say the least, there were some lofty expectations of Harrison and a few other young stars in Golden State. All of this, accompanied by a couple of veterans like Jarrett Jack and Carl Landry, sounded very promising. It was also the first chance for second-year Head Coach Mark Jackson to mentor an injury-free Steph Curry.

During the summer break, Curry had signed a new contract with the Warriors that would keep him in the city until the 2016-17 season. The contract proved that the Warriors meant business and wanted to build their franchise around Curry. The four-year deal was worth $44 million and it went into effect for the 2013-2014 season. Many analysts believe that the Warriors received a great bargain in signing their star player. Tiago Splitter, JaVale McGee, and DeAndre Jordan are just a few players that make more than Curry on a similar contract. In fact, Curry is not even the highest paid player on the roster (Iguodala, Lee, and Bogut currently have higher annual salaries). Curry's history of ankle injuries and his willingness to accept an offer that enabled the Warriors to bring in a big-name free agent for next season are considered to be the main reasons why the contract was significantly below market value for a player of his caliber.

Curry looked like he had real focus at the start of the 2012-2013 season and there was great team chemistry under the guidance of Mark Jackson. That was immediately seen in Curry's game, even though he didn't have the greatest of starts on October 31, 2012, in an 87-85 win at Phoenix. He made just 2 out of 14 from the field and missed all 6 attempts from three-point range for only 5 points – but he did collect 7 rebounds, 3 assists, and 2 steals. Curry began to bounce back in the second game at home with 26 points, making 50 percent from the field overall and 6 for 10 from three-point distance while also collecting 7 assists and 5 rebounds, but the Warriors fell 104-94.

He averaged more than 20 points per game in the first three months of the season and missed only five games due to ankle problems in January. Curry was also putting up a lot more double-doubles than the first three seasons in the NBA, including four in a row in the first half of the season. It started on November 29, 2012, when he scored 20 points with 10 assists, making 7 of 17 field goals (41.2 percent) during a 106-105 win at home over the Denver Nuggets. A few days passed before Curry had another 20 points with 11 assists when he made 50 percent of his shots in a 103-92 win over the Indiana Pacers on December 1, 2012. Curry then finished with 25 points and 11 assists during a 102-94 loss to the Orlando Magic on December 3, 2012. Curry's final part of the four-game double-double streak concluded after he scored 22 points with 10 assists in Golden State's 104-97 win in Detroit on December 5, 2012. It ended when he collected only 5 assists and 4 rebounds on December 7, 2012, in a 109-102 win on the road over the Brooklyn Nets. He did make 10 of 19 from the field (52.6 percent), 5 of 9 from behind the three-point arc (55.6 percent), to finish with 28 points in that game.

January was a good month for Curry with a few big games, beginning on January 2, 2013, during a dominant 115-94 win over the Los Angeles Clippers, in which Curry scored 31 points by converting 11 of 16 total field goal attempts (68.8 percent) while making 6 of 8 from three-point range (75 percent); he also collected 8 assists and 6 rebounds. A little more than a week later, on January 11, 2013, during a 103-97 win over the Portland Trail Blazers, Curry recorded another double-double with 22 points and 12 assists despite only making 31.8 percent of his total field goals. After missing a couple of games due to minor injuries, Curry returned for consecutive wins that featured a tough win at home on January 23, 2013, against the Oklahoma City Thunder by a score of 104-99. In that victory, Curry went 11 of 27 from the field (40.7 percent) to finish with 31 points, along with 7 assists, 4 steals, and 3 rebounds.

He exploded that February with averages of 25.4 points and 6.9 assists, starting on February 2, 2013, after missing a couple more games due to minor pains. In his first game back after a short break, Curry scored on 11 of 20 field goal attempts (55 percent), including 6 of 10 three-pointers, to finish with 29 points plus 8 assists, 2 rebounds, and 2 steals during a 113-93 win at home over the Phoenix Suns. Less than a week later, on February 8, 2013, the Warriors lost 99-93 on the road to the Memphis Grizzlies although Curry converted on 11 of 22 field goals and all 6 free throws to finish the game with 32 points, 8 assists, 5 rebounds, and 2 steals. This included a monumental performance against the New York Knicks at Madison Square Garden in New York City, New York, when he netted a career-high 54 points with 11 of 13 shooting from behind the three-point arc and 18 out of 28 overall from the field – he also had 7 assists, 6 rebounds, and 3 steals in the 109-105 loss on February 27, 2013. The 11 three-pointers in the game brought him in second place on the all-time leading list, him behind Bryant and Donyell Marshall, who had 12 three-pointers in a single game. This came right after Curry scored 38 points by making 14 of 20 in the field and 7 of 10 from three-point range to go along with 4 assists, 3 steals, 2 rebounds, and 1 block during a 108-97 loss to the Indiana Pacers. To say the least, Curry was easily loving how he was performing in the month of February.

But March wasn't a bad month either, as Curry scored 25 points with 6 assists in a 94-86 loss to the Boston Celtics on March 1, 2013. Curry's misfortunes on the road continued in Philadelphia when the Warriors lost to the 76ers, 104-97, on March 2, 2013; he made 11 of 20 from the field to score 30 points while also collecting 9 assists in a near double-double. Curry recorded a double-double with 26 points, 12 assists, and 5 rebounds while converting on 8 of 16 field goals (50 percent) for a 125-118 win over the Toronto Raptors on March 4, 2013, that snapped a four-game losing streak. After a few near double-doubles against the Sacramento Kings and the Houston Rockets, Curry scored 16 points while collecting 10 assists, but he made just 7 of 18 from the field (38.9 percent) in a 103-93 loss at home to the Milwaukee Bucks on March 9, 2013; Curry and the Warriors lost to former Golden State star Monta Ellis, who had 26 points in the game, making 52.6 percent from the field himself. But the thing about Curry is that his struggles were not a long-term problem as he had two big bounce-back games shortly after the loss to the Bucks.

During a 92-63 win over the New York Knicks on March 11, 2013, Curry had a more efficient evening of shooting, making 9 of 18 from the field (which included 6 of 10 from behind the three-point line) to score 26 points with 6 rebounds, 3 assists, and 1 steal. Two nights later, on March 13, 2013, Curry scored 31 points with 8 assists, converting 11 of 17 field goals (64.7 percent), – including 5 of 7 from three-point range – to help Golden State earn a 105-97 win against the Detroit Pistons.

Curry then had one of the worst offensive games of his NBA career on March 15, 2013, when he made just 2 of 13 from the field for 8 points, he had another double-double with 29 points and 11 assists after making 12 of 22 from the field and 5 of 11 three-point field goals during a 108-78 win on the road in Houston on

March 17, 2013. Curry topped that about 24 hours later on March 18, 2013, with 10 of 19 field goals, including 6 of 9 from behind the three-point arc, to finish with 30 points, 7 rebounds, and 3 assists as the Golden State Warriors won, 93-72, in New Orleans. Less than a week later, Curry scored another 35 points by shooting 72.2 percent from the field, 6 of 10 from three-point range, to go along with 8 assists for the team's 40th win, when they defeated the Washington Wizards by a score of 101-92 on March 23, 2013. The playoff push for the Warriors continued on March 25, 2013, as Curry had a near triple-double with 25 points, 10 assists, and 7 rebounds during Golden State's 109-103 win over the Los Angeles Lakers. He recorded a second consecutive double-double with 17 points and 12 assists in a loss to the Sacramento Kings on March 30, 2013.

Curry continued to keep his scoring average above 20 points per game in the month of April, through the final games of the regular season, as Golden State hoped to solidify a spot in the 2013 NBA Playoffs. During a 98-88 win against the New Orleans Hornets on April 3, 2013, Curry shot 42.9 percent from the field for 20 points with 9 assists, 3 rebounds, and a steal. Curry then recorded a double-double with a season-high 15 assists and 18 points although he a below-average 40 percent shooting night (6 of 15 field goals), as the Warriors got a critical road win over the Phoenix Suns on April 5, 2013. After Curry scored 22 points on 8 of 19 field goal attempts in a 97-90 loss to the Utah Jazz on April 7, 2013, he recorded yet another double-digit number of assists with 10 and scored 24 points, making 9 of 21 field goals (42.9 percent) during a 105-89 win against the Minnesota Timberwolves.

He also had a 47-point game against Kobe Bryant and the Los Angeles Lakers on April 12, 2013. Although it was a 118-116 loss at the Staples Center in Los Angeles, California, Curry went 17 of 31 from the field (54.8 percent) – including 9 out of 15 from three-point range (60 percent) – while also collecting 9 assists, 6 rebounds, and 3 steals. But these individual game numbers were not enough for Curry, as he looked determined to break a more significant and more recent all-time record. That finally happened at the end of the season when he broke Ray Allen's record of total three-pointers in one season, scoring 272 times from beyond the arc while playing in just 78 games. By the end of the year, Curry had probably made that $44 million contract the "bargain of the century," based on his outstanding season.

Curry finished the 2012-2013 regular season averaging 22.9 points, 4 rebounds, 6.9 assists, and 1.6 steals while shooting with 45.3 percent accuracy from three-point land and 45.1 percent from the field overall. Curry won the Western Conference Player of the Month award for April, in which he averaged 25.4 points, 8.1 assists, 3.9 rebounds, and 2.1 steals with a field goal percentage of 46.5. He earned praise from Head Coach Mark Jackson for being half of the most intimidating backcourt shooting duo in NBA history, also known as the "Splash Brothers" (with Klay Thompson as the other half of the duo). This was the season when Curry became an All-Star quality guard and led the Warriors to their first playoff appearance in his era. They finished with a record of 47-35, good for second place in the Pacific Division behind the Los Angeles Clippers (56-26). That was good enough to clinch the sixth spot in the very competitive Western Conference playoffs. The West was much more competitive than the Eastern Conference, where the final eighth seed was the 38-44 Milwaukee Bucks.

The sixth-seeded Warriors were matched up against the third-seeded Denver Nuggets in the opening round of the playoffs, with the Nuggets winning the first game by a narrow score of 97-95 on April 20, 2013; Curry converted just 7 of 20 from the field (35 percent) for 19 points, with 9 assists, 4 rebounds, and 2 steals. But the Splash Brothers made, well, a splash in a 131-117 win in Game 2 on April 23, 2013; Curry made 13 of 23 from the field (56.5 percent) and 4 of 10 from three-point range for 30 points, 13 assists, 5 rebounds, and 3 steals. Thompson was 8 of 11 from the field (72.7 percent) and a near perfect 5 of 6 on three-point field goal attempts for 21 points of his own. Golden State returned home for a Game 3 win on April 26, 2013, by a 110-108 score, with Curry's 29 points leading the team; he also had 11 assists, 6 rebounds, and 2 steals while making 6 of 17 from the field (4 of 7 for 3 points) and 4 of 4 on the foul line. The winning continued in Game 4 on April 28, 2013, as the Warriors earned a 115-101 win over Denver. In that victory, Curry made 10 of 16 (62.5 percent) from the field, 6 of 11 (54.5 percent) from behind the three-point arc, and a perfect 5 of 5 in free throws for 31 points, along with 7 assists, 4 steals, and 3 rebounds.

The Nuggets wouldn't go away easily as they took Game 5 in Denver, Colorado, on April 30, 2013, with a 107-100 win in which Curry was limited to just 15 points, 8 assists, and 4 rebounds; he made just 7 of 19 from the field for 36.8 percent. But Golden State closed out the series with a Game 6 win, 92-88, at home on May 2, 2013. Curry made 42.9 percent from the field overall with 4 of 8 from three-point range and all 6 free throws to finish the game with 22 points, 8 assists, 4 rebounds, and 2 steals. Curry almost singlehandedly eliminated the Nuggets in six games averaging 24.3 points, 9.3 assists, 4.3 rebounds, 2.2 steals while shooting 47 percent from the field. NBA media praised Curry as the Most Valuable Player of the playoffs because of his ridiculous stats and the fact that he had so much impact on his team while on the floor.

The Warriors faced the experienced San Antonio Spurs in the second round of the playoffs. The Spurs had gone 58-24 to win the

NBA's Southwest Division Championship. Curry scored 44 points with 11 assists, 4 rebounds, and 2 steals while making 18 of 35 from the field (51.4 percent), the top-notch individual performance in a heartbreaking double overtime loss, 129-127, on May 6, 2013. The Warriors tied the series in San Antonio in Game 2 – much like the series against the Denver Nuggets – on May 8, 2013, as Curry scored 22 points to support Thompson's 34 points and 14 rebounds in a 100-91 win. Curry struggled in the Game 3 loss on May 10, 2013, as he made just 5 out of 17 field goals (29.4 percent) for only 16 points with 8 assists in the 102-92 loss. But Golden State forced an overtime thriller on May 12, 2013, as they were able to defeat the Spurs 97-87 after Harrison Barnes led the team with 26 points and 10 rebounds; Curry was second in scoring for Golden State with 22 points, while Andrew Bogut led the team with 18 total rebounds.

Curry averaged nearly 46 minutes per game in the first four meetings of the series, which took a big toll on his performance in Game 5, when he scored only 9 points and had 4 turnovers as the Spurs jumped ahead in the series 3-2 with a 109-91 win on May 14, 2013. Curry made just 4 of 14 from the field for 28.6 percent and only 1 of 7 three-point attempts. The Spurs went on to win the series 4-2 by defeating the Warriors in Oakland, California, on May 16, 2013. Curry led the Warriors with 22 points, 6 assists, 4 rebounds, 1 steal, and 1 block while making 10 of 25 from the field and just 2 of 8 from three-point distance. While it was a tough end to the postseason for the Warriors, there was no shame in losing to a Spurs team that continued their postseason run by advancing to the 2013 NBA Finals, where they ultimately lost to the defending champions Miami Heat in a full seven-game series.

Regardless of what happened in the Spurs series, Steph Curry proved that he was the future of the Golden State Warriors and that he was capable of leading his team with the help of his coach, Mark Jackson. The trust of the franchise in Curry when they traded former star Ellis to build the team around him had been validated. It was also a sign for general manager, Bob Myers, to invest even more in the team and to bring another star player to complete the already intimidating starting five. The Golden State Warriors became an even more formidable team when they signed veteran All-Star and versatile small forward Andre Iguodala as a free agent. Iguodala had a reputation of being one of the best passing wingmen in the game and also as a very solid perimeter defender, something the team was in dire need of. This addition created one of the best teams in the league on paper and improved the chances of playoff success for the Warriors in the 2013-2014 season.

2013-14 season[xvi]

With Golden State looking a lot stronger entering the season, it didn't take long for Curry to hit his offensive stride. Despite a 126-

115 loss on the road against the Los Angeles Clippers on October 31, 2013, Curry made 14 of 23 total field goals (60.9 percent) with 9 of 14 made three-point field goals (64.3 percent) for 38 points with 9 assists. But that was mere peanuts to some of the big games Curry put up statistically in the 2013-14 season.

Curry hit the 40-point mark for the first time in the season on December 9, 2013, during a 115-111 loss to the Charlotte Bobcats; he made 14 of 32 field goals (43.8 percent) and 10 of 12 from the foul line for 43 points, with 9 assists, 6 rebounds, and 2 blocks. He surpassed that with 44 points, making 14 of 26 from the field with 8 of 13 from three-point range and 8 of 9 free throws during a 95-90 win over the Utah Jazz on January 31, 2014. But Curry's highest point total for the year was near the end of the regular season on April 13, 2014, during a 119-117 loss on the road to the Portland Trail Blazers – he scored 47 points, making 16 of 29 field goals (55.2 percent) with 7 of 14 from three-point range and all 8 free throws.

During the season, Curry played in 78 games and had a career-high 28 double-doubles; he also had triple-doubles in four games, which was another career high. The first was on November 4, 2013, in a 110-90 win while visiting the Philadelphia 76ers, in which he scored 18 points, with 12 assists and 10 rebounds, shooting 43.8 percent from the field; he also had 5 steals and 1 block. A little more than a month later, on December 27, 2013, Curry had more assists (16) than points (14) and rebounds (13) in a tough night of shooting – 5 of 17 from the field (29.4 percent) – as Golden State defeated the Phoenix Suns 115-86. A couple of months later, Curry had his third triple-double with 27 points, 11 assists, and 11 rebounds during a 126-103 win visiting the New York Knicks on February 28, 2014. The fourth triple-double was his best: He scored 30 points, 12 assists, and 10 rebounds during the Warriors' 112-95 win over the Los Angeles Lakers on April 11, 2014.

Steph Curry continued to lead his team, finishing with averages of 24 points, 8.5 assists (both career highs), and 1.6 steals per game. That was his best season to date, and the Warriors entered the playoffs again after Golden State finished with a record of 51-31, finished behind the Los Angeles Clippers for the Pacific Division crown, as the Clippers won 57 games. The Warriors were the sixth spot again and faced the Clippers in the first round of the playoffs. It was an interesting matchup between the two most successful players from the 2009 NBA draft class: Blake Griffin and Steph Curry.

The Warriors took the first game in Los Angeles with a 109-105 win on April 19, 2014; Thompson led the team with 22 points and Lee recorded a double-double with 20 points and 13 rebounds, while Curry struggled offensively with 6 of 16 shooting for 37.5 percent and 14 points to go with 7 assists and 3 steals. The Clippers avenged the loss in Game 2 on April 21, 2014, as Curry was the lone offensive ray of hope with 24 points, converting on 52.9 percent from the field – but he made just 1 of 7 from three-point range. Curry had a tough night shooting in Game 3 on April 24, 2014, with just 5 of 12 shooting (41.7 percent) from the field for 16 points with 15 assists during a 98-96 loss at home to the Clippers to fall 2-1 in the first-round series.

But, as mentioned before, Curry doesn't shoot cold for long periods of time. During Game 4 on April 27, 2014, he made 10 of 20 field goals, including 7 of 14 from three-point range, with 6 of 7 from the foul line for 33 points, plus 7 rebounds and 7 assists to give the Warriors the series-tying 118-97 win. After the Clippers took Game 5 with a 113-103 decision to go ahead 3-2, Curry led the team with 24 points, 9 assists, and 4 rebounds in a 100-99 win on May 1, 2014, to avoid elimination. In a hard-fought and very controversial series, Griffin's Clippers managed to edge out Curry's Warriors in 7 games. The Clippers closed out the series with a 126-121 win on May 3, 2014. Curry had a valiant effort with 7 of 17 field goals (41.2 percent) and made all 16 attempts from the foul line to score 33 points with 9 assists, 5 rebounds, and 3 steals.

Both Curry and Griffin had tremendous seasons and have become true leaders of their teams. Curry managed to record the second triple-double of his career, to stay injury-free for the whole season, and to participate in the All-Star Game after being voted by the fans as their second choice in the West, behind Kevin Durant. Curry set another record during the season by making 261 three-pointers which, coupled with his record-setting 272 the year before, gave him the record for the most three-pointers made in a span of two seasons with 533. In addition, he and Klay Thompson set the record for most combined threes in a year with 484. These two really lived up to their nickname, the "Splash Brothers". Curry was also named to the All-NBA Second Team for the first time, further cementing his status as one of the top players in the league today.

2014 All-Star Game

Curry was selected as a starter for the 2014 NBA All-Star Game. It was his first appearance in his five-year career. Curry placed second behind Kevin Durant in fan voting for the Western Conference starters. It was a great accomplishment for him and a lot of buzz circulated a week before the game as everyone was talking about his sweet jump shot and three-point range. Even the President of the United States, Barack Obama, stated in an interview that Curry is the best shooter he has ever seen, including Chicago's South Side legends. Curry was the first All-Star starter for Golden State since Latrell Sprewell in the 1995 All-Star Game and the first vote leader for a position since Rick Barry in 1976.

Curry started the All-Star Game and missed 9 three-point shots of 10 attempts. He only managed to score 12 points in the game.

Noticing that he was cold from the floor, Curry focused on setting up his teammates instead. He dished 11 assists and helped Durant and Blake Griffin score 76 points combined, in the highest scoring All-Star Game of all time. He also had one nice behind-the-back and through-the-legs dribble that sent LeBron James and James Harden chasing after his ghost. After the game, Curry said that his bad shooting performance was partly due to long game breaks between timeouts and quarters. The East won the game after a three-year drought and fellow point guard Kyrie Irving was named the Most Valuable Player.

The All-Star Game showed the world that Curry had developed into a more versatile player after his 2012-13 breakout season and his stats support that statement. He set personal highs in points, assists, and free throw attempts per 36 minutes of play during the season. The assist rate, which measures possessions that ended with an assist from Curry, increased significantly to 41%. But the improvement in passing was not the only offense for the 25-year-old product of Davidson. Curry also improved his defense by limiting his foul rate and producing a defensive rating of 102. Curry's importance to the team is shown by the fact that Golden State was outscored by 7 points when he was on the bench.

2014-15 Offseason and Early Season[xvii]

Despite leading the Warriors to consecutive playoff appearances, Mark Jackson was fired just three days after their first-round exit at the hands of the Clippers. The players publicly voiced their support for Jackson, but ownership had seemingly made up their mind as reports of dysfunction in the team's coaching staff came out before their playoff run. Assistant Coach Brian Scalabrine was reassigned to Santa Cruz, the team's D-League affiliate because of "philosophical differences" with Jackson, and two weeks later another assistant, Darren Erman, was fired because he secretly recorded conversations between coaches, staff, and players. The firing of Jackson, even though he instigated the turnaround of the franchise, showed the fickle nature of head coaching jobs in the NBA. He was a master motivator and helped to immensely improve Golden State's once non-existent defense. However, many observers felt that Jackson's offensive sets were too stagnant and led to isolation plays most of the time. He didn't use Curry as an off-the-ball shooter that much and also failed to utilize Andrew Bogut's fine passing skills from the post.

The head honchos of the team were looking for a different direction and on May 14, 2014, they announced the hiring of TNT analyst Steve Kerr to a five-year contract reportedly worth 25 million dollars. Kerr had won multiple titles with the Chicago Bulls and San Antonio Spurs as a player before serving as the

President and General Manager of the Phoenix Suns from 2007-10. Kerr owns the NBA record for career three-point percentage with a clip of 45.5 percent. Curry was one of the most vocal supporters of Jackson, but the appointment of one of the best three-point shooters of all time and an offensive-minded coach in Kerr could potentially lead to maximizing the potential of one of the league's most potent offenses, and even improve Curry's individual game as well.

The Warriors made some minor moves in the offseason, including the signing of combo guards Shaun Livingston and Leandro Barbosa to be the relievers of the "Splash Brothers," further strengthening the Warriors' already powerhouse backcourt. But perhaps the biggest move of the summer for the Golden State Warriors was not giving up Curry's Splash Brother Klay Thompson in exchange for Kevin Love.

Before the Cleveland Cavaliers got Love via trade, the Golden State Warriors was one of the teams that were actively involved in the Kevin Love sweepstakes. But Love's former team, the Minnesota Timberwolves, was only interested in discussing the trade with the Warriors if the latter included Klay Thompson in their trade proposal. However, instead of getting lured into getting the sharpshooting Love as their new power forward, the Warriors believed that keeping the Splash Brothers intact and making them the cornerstones of the team was the right way to move forward.

Golden State then went on to re-sign Thompson to a four-year $70M contract extension.

Keeping Thompson was a no-brainer although the temptation of getting a three-point shooting and rebounding demon in Kevin Love was a tricky situation. If the Warriors had acquired Love, the whole offensive scheme would have changed with a new threat in the frontcourt. However, keeping Curry and Thompson together meant the continuity of the young core and the development of a backcourt that was emerging as one of the NBA's best, especially after their participation in the gold-winning performance of Team USA in the 2014 FIBA Basketball World Cup in Spain.

The Splash Brothers' performance in the 2014 FIBA Basketball World Cup proved the value of both Curry and Thompson as individual basketball players and affirmed the Warriors' decision to keep the pair together. While it was only Stephen Curry who started all of Team USA's games, Klay Thompson's streaky shooting and tough perimeter defense often led the mid-game spurts and little runs that broke games wide open for the Americans. Sure, it was Cleveland Cavaliers guard Kyrie Irving who was named the tournament MVP in the 2014 FIBA Basketball World Cup, but the contributions of both Curry and Thompson were invaluable in winning the gold medal. On the side of the players, the impact of playing for the flag went way beyond the statistics that they produced.

Curry and Thompson returned to the Warriors more confident than ever and eager to prove themselves on the NBA stage too. And why not? After conquering the world stage and winning the gold medal for their country, the next challenge to accomplish was winning the NBA title.

The hiring of Steve Kerr as coach was the first move in that championship direction because, as the former designated shooter for both the Chicago Bulls and San Antonio Spurs during some of their championship runs, Kerr had a grasp, on a first-person level, of the value of shooters and the three-point shot to the game and to a successful title run. And rightfully so, because Kerr hit one big three-point shot after another for those two teams during his NBA career. So with a coach who fully understood their game and value to the team, it was only a matter of time before the Splash Brothers played beautiful music with their older Splash Brother in Coach Steve Kerr.

Early on during the regular season, Kerr's coaching philosophy seemed to work wonders for the team and Curry as Golden State got off to a scorching 8-2 start to lead the Pacific Division. Two wins later and after defeating the Oklahoma City Thunder on November 23, the 10-2 Warriors had the best start in franchise history. They did not stop winning.

Stephen Curry averaged 27.5 points and 4 three-pointers per game in the next four games to finish the month of November on a high note. And because all four were road games, the Warriors scored their first perfect road trip (5-0) since 1978 and only the second spotless away trip in franchise history.

Kerr had added more variation to the Warriors' offensive patterns, such as running the offense through Australian center Andrew Bogut more than in the previous years and allowing Bogut to create plays from the post, letting Klay Thompson facilitate the offense, and relieving Curry of the ball-handling duties from time to time. Kerr's system brought the best out of Bogut and Thompson, who showed that he is also a very adept penetrator, not just a spot-up shooter and a premier perimeter defender. Still, it was not only on offense where they were good, as the Warriors also showed tremendous improvement in their defensive efficiency, demonstrating that Kerr also emphasized on the other side of the game. More important, Curry began to flourish in Kerr's system by averaging 23.8 points, 4.9 rebounds, 7.9 assists, 3.26 three-pointers made per game, and very efficient shooting percentages of 50.2% from the field and 92.8% from the free throw line during the month of November. The new system did wonders for Curry's offense, allowing him to come off screens set by his teammates and imitating some of the sets that the Atlanta Hawks used to free up their own sharpshooter, Kyle Korver.

Curry's game wasn't the only thing that was getting better by the day, but his relationship with Steve Kerr improved as well. Curry and his coach even engaged in shooting contests just to keep the Warriors' point guard sharp at all times. This started with the highly publicized free throw shooting contest between player and coach during the preseason. In that much documented video, Curry beat his coach by a single point. The friendly competition between player and coach did not end there. It was followed by a couple more foul shooting contests and even a three-point contest which almost mimicked the one that Curry had with former Head Coach Mark Jackson in the previous season. Slowly, Kerr gained Curry's trust and it was mutual. With the relationship between star player and coach going very well, the Warriors started the season like a house on fire.

As November came to a close, the 14-2 Warriors were the NBA's surprise leaders in a season where injuries altered the experts' predictions. The defending champion San Antonio Spurs, who returned with their 2014 championship lineup intact, were seen as favorites to repeat and rule the Western Conference. However, injuries to key players like Kawhi Leonard, Tony Parker, and Manu Ginobili forced the Spurs to struggle after the first full month of the 2015 season. Along with the Spurs, the other 2014 Western Conference finalist Oklahoma City Thunder suffered a big blow when 2014 MVP Kevin Durant started the season on the sideline after suffering a Jones fracture and undergoing surgery during the offseason. During their first game of the 2015 regular season, Durant's sidekick Russell Westbrook injured his hand and he too was out of the Thunder lineup in November. With these two title favorites hurting and the Los Angeles Clippers struggling to find their form, the fast start gave Curry and the Warriors more confidence to push further into the tough Western Conference.

By December 10, 2014, the Warriors' winning streak had extended to 14 games, giving them the longest winning streak in franchise history. This record was extended to 16 before the Warriors lost to their eventual second-round playoff opponents, the Memphis Grizzlies, on December 16 in Memphis. On January 7, 2015, Curry became the fastest player in NBA history to make 1,000 career three-point baskets. He accomplished the feat in 369 games, which was 88 games faster than the previous record of 457 games set by former Orlando Magic three-point specialist Dennis Scott. Two weeks later, Curry and the Warriors established a new franchise record for consecutive home wins at 17. They added two more before losing to the Chicago Bulls on January 27, 2015. The loss to the Bulls proved to be the team's final home loss of the regular season.

On January 23, 2015, Curry's Splash Brother Klay Thompson exploded for a career-high 52 points against the Sacramento Kings in a 126-101 blowout that gave the team a franchise best and league-leading 35-6 start. During that game, Thompson set the record for most points in a single quarter with 37 during the third period of that game. He broke the previous record of 33 points, which was shared by George Gervin and Carmelo Anthony.

But more than Klay Thompson breaking that record and setting a career high in points scored in a single game, it was Stephen Curry's unselfishness that made that game more memorable. With Thompson scorching hot, Curry took just 11 shots in the entire game, 5.8 attempts fewer than his season average and scored just 10 points. Those 10 points later turned out to be Curry's third lowest scoring game of the season, and it wasn't because he was struggling so much from the field or that he was being defended very well by the opposition. Rather, it was because he took the backseat and allowed Klay Thompson to grab the spotlight on the biggest night of his NBA career. Curry also finished the game with 11 assists, mostly to Thompson, who went 13-13 from the field during the record-breaking third quarter.

Curry's basketball actions during that game proved once and for all that there is no sibling rivalry between the Splash Brothers because they genuinely like each other as persons and players. Instead of competing for the limelight, they feed off each other and push each other to do things better. And because of this harmony, Curry and Thompson became the destructive offensive duo that has propelled the Golden State Warriors to new heights in 2015.

Two weeks later, Curry proved that harmony and returned the favor to Thompson by putting up his best offensive output of the season, scoring 51 points in a 128-114 destruction of the Dallas Mavericks on February 4, 2015. Curry went berserk from the floor, hitting 16 of 26 shots from the field, including 10 of 16 from three-point distance, as the Warriors erased a 42-25 first quarter deficit to win and improve their league-leading record to 39-8.

Curry poured in 26 points in the third quarter alone as the Dubs took the lead for good against the Mavericks. He looked unstoppable and hit three-pointers from as far as three to four feet behind the three-point line. Curry's 51-point effort gave the Splash Brothers yet another NBA record as their Golden State Warriors became just the seventh team in NBA history to have two different players score at least 50 points in a game in the same season.

At the end of the first month of 2015, the 37-8 Warriors had a comfortable lead over their Western Conference rivals and had established themselves as the surprise team to beat in the West just as the Atlanta Hawks were in the East. Curry led the team in scoring in 19 of their total games and already had eight 30-plus scoring nights by January 2015. He also led the Warriors in assists in all but five games up to that point.

Steph Curry had played in the entire Warriors' 45 regular-season games by January 31, 2015, and he was averaging 23.0 points, 8.1

assists, 4.7 rebounds, and 2.1 steals per game, all better than his career averages. He was also making 3 three-pointers per game at a high 39.5 percent clip and was shooting a league-best 91.5% from the foul line heading into the midway point of the season.

The 2015 All-Star Weekend

As word of the Warriors' emergence spread, Stephen Curry's legend also started to grow. When the first set of fan votes for the 2015 NBA All-Star Games was announced, Curry topped the list for the Western Conference with 549,095 votes. Out East, it was three-time top vote-getter LeBron James leading the way with a league-best 552,967 votes. But while everyone expected James to be on top of the list, nobody expected that Steph Curry would surpass former three-time leading vote-getter Kobe Bryant of the Los Angeles Lakers in the Western Conference.

Bryant last led the NBA balloting in 2013 but had missed out on the All-Star Game the previous season because of injury. The five-time NBA champion had been the yardstick for NBA guards and one of its best offensive weapons. However, Bryant was struggling on a team composed of journeymen and untested youngsters. On the other hand, Curry and the Warriors were creating a recipe for success. The initial tally was perhaps the proverbial changing of the guard in the Western Conference.

When the second wave of votes was counted, James seemed to be on his way to his fourth number one finish in the fan balloting, as he led Curry by around 14,000 votes. But when the final count was announced on January 22, Curry had overtaken James as the top vote-getter for the 2015 All-Star Game, amassing a total of 1,513,324 votes, compared to James' runner-up finish of 1,470,483 votes. With that, Curry not only earned his second All-Star Game appearance but he also became the first Warriors player to start in back-to-back All-Star games since Chris Mullin in 1991-1992. He also officially became the most popular player in the NBA by dethroning the NBA's King, LeBron James, who was the previous year's top vote-getter.

However, topping the All-Star Game voting and starting for the Western Conference wasn't Curry's main goal for the 2015 All-Star Weekend; returning to the three-point contest was.

As the league's premier three-point gunner, it was but academic that Curry would enter the contest which he had been dying to win since 2010. It will be recalled that Curry topped the first round of the three-point contest in the 2010 All-Star Weekend but lost to Paul Pierce in the finals. Curry skipped the event the next two seasons and participated again in 2013 and 2014. However, he didn't get past the first round in either instance. Frustrated, Curry vowed to compete in the three-point contest until he won it.

Curry entered himself in the 2015 contest, but he wasn't the only top gun who enlisted in the competition. Five other players who were in the season's top 10 for three-point field goals made also joined the contest. The eight-man cast was completed by the winners of the previous two seasons: defending champion Marco Belinelli of the San Antonio Spurs and Kyrie Irving of the Cavs, who had won the competition in 2013.

The other competitors were Kyle Korver of the Atlanta Hawks, who was then having a run at a historic 50-50-90 shooting season; the Rockets' James Harden; first-time competitor but perennial three-point threat J.J. Redick; the Portland Trailblazers' All-time three-point leader, Wesley Matthews; and Curry's fellow Splash Brother, Klay Thompson.

Curry was one of the favorites, but all the pressure was on him because, if he had lost that contest, he would have joined the likes of Reggie Miller (five times), Dana Barros (four times), and current Boston Celtics GM Danny Ainge (four times) as the only players to enter the contest at least four times without winning. That pressure though was nothing new and Curry said he felt that this was his year. He was correct.

Although the competition was impressive and top-notch, Curry easily entered the final round with 23 points and was joined there by Kyrie Irving (who also had 23) and teammate Klay Thompson, who topped the first round with 24 markers.

Curry was the first to shoot in the final round, followed by Irving and then Thompson. But after Curry was done with his 60-second final round, it was clear that he set the bar too high for his opponents. He dazzled the crowd and shot the lights out of the Barclay's Center by scoring 27 out of a possible 34 points in a fantastic shooting display. Thompson finished second with 17 points, while Irving came up third with 14 points.

Two nights later, Curry and Thompson helped lead the Western Conference All-Stars to a 161-158 win over their Eastern counterparts. Curry tallied 15 points, 9 rebounds, and 5 spectacular assists in 26:36 minutes while Thompson added 7 points, 4 rebounds, and 6 assists in 19:43 of action. And while it was Russell Westbrook of the OKC Thunder who was named the All-Star Game MVP after scoring 44 points, the Splash Brothers stamped their class on the 2015 All-Star Weekend and served notice to the entire league that they would be a force to reckon with when the second half of the season begins.

Best Record in the NBA[xviii]

On March 24, 2015, the Warriors clinched the Pacific Division title for the first time since 1976 with a win over the Portland Trail Blazers. On that same night, they also established the franchise record for most road wins in a single season with their 24th win away from the Oracle Center. On March 28, the Warriors set another franchise record for most wins in a single season with 60 wins. Win number 60 also assured the Warriors of home-court advantage until the Western Conference Finals. They went on to break their franchise record for most wins seven more times and ended the season with the best record in the entire league at 67-15, becoming only the 10th team in NBA history to win at least 67 games. In doing so, the Warriors claimed home-court advantage for the entire 2015 postseason as they hoped to replicate their regular-season success in the playoffs, where they hadn't had much success in the past.

Before the Warriors' 2013 playoff appearance, they had missed the big dance for five straight years, including Curry's first three seasons in the NBA. In Curry's six seasons in the NBA, he'd seen the playoffs only in the past three seasons and his first two cracks at the postseason both ended in first-round defeats. But this season was different because the Warriors broke one franchise record after another.

The Warriors had a first-time coach in Steve Kerr, who broke the record for most wins by a coach in his first season in the NBA. Like his team and coach, Stephen Curry also broke several records during the 2015 season.

Aside from breaking his record for most three-pointers in a single season, Curry and Thompson also obliterated their own record for most three-pointers combined by two teammates with 525. The Splash Brothers had set the former record of 484 the previous season.

Curry finished the season sixth in scoring (23.8 PPG), sixth in assists (7.7 APG), and fourth in steals (2.04 SPG) and had a career-best 4.3 rebounds per game. His 44.3% conversion from the three-point area was also fourth in the NBA, while his 91.4% free throw shooting percentage was the best in the league. Curry also made a career-high 52 straight foul shots without a miss from March 9 to April 4, 2015.

With these record-shattering performances on both the team and individual level, Stephen Curry erased all the criticisms that had been pasted on his back: weak ankles, poor defense and the inability to finish around the basket. He isn't the freight train that LeBron James is or the complete greatness that Michael Jordan was. But he dominated the season in his own way: shooting threes like we've never seen before. He changed the geography of pro basketball by putting a premium on the three-point shot more than any other player in its history. With all the accomplishments he reached that season, Curry was no longer the future of the NBA; his time had arrived.

The MVP[xix]

With the Golden State Warriors emerging as the league leader in the NBA team standings for the 2015 season, Stephen Curry's name began appearing in MVP discussions and deservedly so, because he was the motor that ran the best team in the league. But Curry wasn't the only player who was having a standout season.

The New Orleans Pelicans' power forward Anthony Davis emerged as one of the top big men in the NBA with a breakout 2015 season. The first overall pick of the 2012 NBA draft was fourth in the NBA in scoring (24.4 PPG), eighth in rebounding (10.2 RPG), and number one in shot blocks (2.94 BPG).

Oklahoma City's ferocious floor general Russell Westbrook also had an incredible season, recording 11 triple-doubles. Westbrook achieved a rare feat by recording consecutive triple-doubles four games in a row – the last player to do that was Michael Jordan in the 1990s – and an impressive six over an eight-game span. Westbrook also became the seventh player in league history to have at least 10 triple-doubles in a single season since 1985-86.

But Westbrook's Thunder was struggling with Kevin Durant injured, as were Davis' Pelicans because of the injuries to starting PG Jrue Holiday and sweet shooting forward Ryan Anderson. With their teams struggling, Westbrook's and Davis's MVP bid were both in jeopardy, as 21 of the last 24 regular-season MVPs had come from teams with top the records and, since 1982, the NBA's regular-season MVP has come from a team with at least 50 wins.

That piece of historical data theoretically narrowed down the MVP conversation to Stephen Curry and James Harden, whose Houston Rockets were surging in the second half of the season even without All-Star center Dwight Howard for a handful of games due to a knee injury.

Harden, who incidentally was a teammate of Curry and Anthony Davis on the US Men's basketball team to the 2014 FIBA Basketball World Cup, was also having a career season. Harden's 2015 season averages of 27.4 points, 5.7 rebounds, 7.0 assists, 1.9 steals, and 0.7 blocks were all career highs. The player popularly known as "The Beard" had 10 40-point games and 33 30-point games in 81 regular-season games played. He became the first player in the Houston Rockets' franchise history to have two 50-point games in a single season. He also led the Rockets to their first division title since 1994.

But what made Harden's 2015 season really impressive was the fact that he was able to accomplish all these without Dwight Howard for a total of 41 games because of a knee injury. On the other hand, Stephen Curry had a very talented team around him that helped him get the victories for Golden State. Nevertheless,

Curry was named the 2015 NBA MVP shortly before the Warriors played Game 2 of their second-round series against the Memphis Grizzlies.

Statistically, Curry was truly the Warriors' MVP. He was a plus 11.5 points for his team during his 80 games in the regular season. Overall, the Warriors scored 920 more points than their opponents when Curry was on the floor.

Curry received 100 out of 130 first-place votes from a panel consisting of 129 sportswriters and broadcasters plus one vote coming from a fan poll on NBA.com. As expected, Harden came in second with 25 first-place votes while four-time MVP LeBron James finished in third place with five first-place votes. Rounding out the top 5 were Westbrook and Davis.

Curry became the Warriors' first MVP winner since Wilt Chamberlain in 1960, back when the Warriors were still playing for Philadelphia. He also became the second player in league history to win the MVP and play for a team with 65 wins. The only other player to achieve that feat was Earvin "Magic" Johnson in 1987, when Magic led the Lakers to the 1987 NBA title. But will lightning strike twice with Curry and the Warriors?

2015 NBA Playoffs[xx]

After opening the season with 20-to-1 odds to win the NBA title in the Las Vegas Superbook, the top-seeded Golden State Warriors started the 2015 postseason as the top title favorites, along with LeBron James and his Cleveland Cavaliers.

Steph Curry found himself playing against FIBA World Cup teammate and fellow MVP contender Anthony Davis in the first round of the playoffs. Davis willed his New Orleans Pelicans to the playoffs by edging out the Russell Westbrook-fueled Oklahoma City Thunder on the final day of the regular season – April 15, 2015 – by way of a 108-103 upset win over the San Antonio Spurs. In contrast, the Warriors and Curry had already sealed home-court advantage a couple of weeks earlier as they finished with a record of 67-15. Their matchup looked like a classic battle between David and Goliath, except that the little Stephen Curry was the Goliath while the long and lanky Anthony Davis was the David.

Curry led the Warriors to a 106-99 win over the Pelicans in Game 1 on April 18, 2015. Although the final score was close, it didn't show the fact that Steph Curry dominated the majority of the game despite shooting just 4 of 13 from three-point distance. Curry shot 13 of 25 from the field and scored a total of 34 points as his Warriors led 84-66 at the start of the fourth quarter. Davis scored

20 of his 35 points in the final period to lead a furious Pelicans' rally, but Curry and the Warriors held on to win the opener.

The Pelicans opened Game 2 strong on April 20, 2015, and held a 13-point lead in the first quarter before the Warriors exploded in the second period to take the lead for good. The Warriors leaned on Klay Thompson's 26 points and Curry's 22 markers, which featured plus 6 assists, to beat the Pelicans 97-87 and take a 2-0 lead to Game 3 in New Orleans. But if we thought that the Warriors' second-quarter comeback in Game 2 was impressive, Steph Curry pulled a rabbit out of his magical hat in a Game 3 performance that was one for the ages.

Down by 20 to start the fourth quarter and behind by 17 points with six minutes left to play, Curry spearheaded one of the most spectacular comebacks in NBA playoff history, was punctuated by a miraculous three-pointer from 24 feet away with three seconds left that sent the game into overtime. In the extra period, Curry hit the first basket of the overtime – another three-pointer from about 26 feet away – that gave the Warriors a lead that they never relinquished in that character-defining 123-119 Game 3 win in New Orleans on April 23, 2015. Again, Curry struggled from the field, shooting just 10-29 of his shots which included a playoff record-tying 18 three-point attempts (with just 8 connections). But he not only scored a game-high 40 points (along with 9 assists and 5 rebounds), he also hit one big basket after another and those clutch buckets finished the Pelicans, not just in Game 3 but throughout the series.

Still shocked after their Game 3 collapse, the Pelicans got swept in Game 4 on April 25, 2015, by a score of 109-98. Curry led the Warriors once again with 39 points on 11 of 20 shooting from the field while also collecting another 9 assists, 8 rebounds, and 1 steal. He made 7 of 11 on uncontested shots as the Warriors advanced to Round 2 of the playoffs for only the third time since 1991.

With Mike Conley sitting out Game 1 to recover from surgery to repair broken facial bones, the Warriors picked up where they left off and shrugged off eight days of inactivity to roll to a 101-86 series opener win on May 3, 2015. The Warriors' win came behind Curry's 22 points, 7 assists, and 4 steals, while he made just 44.4 percent of his field goal attempts. But just as everyone thought Curry and the Warriors steamrolled past the Grizzlies, the team with the motto "Grit and Grind" did what only two other teams have done during the season.

The Grizzlies beat the Warriors at the Oracle Arena on May 5, 2015. The Warriors entered Game 2 with a 21-game home winning streak and a record of 42-2 at home this season. However, the return of a masked Mike Conley inspired the Grizzlies. Conley hit his first 4 shots and outdueled Curry to give Memphis a 97-90 win and deal the Warriors their first home loss since January 27, 2015.

More importantly, the Grizzlies stole home-court advantage and headed home for Game 3 oozing with confidence. Curry struggled in Game 3 with Memphis' defense swarming him like a slew of hungry bears. Collectively, the Warriors went 12 of 31 on open shots while Curry shot just 8 of 21 from the field and 2 of 10 from three-point range, one game after going 7 of 19 from the floor and 2 of 11 from three-point land. For the first time in the 2015 season, the Warriors looked very vulnerable and Memphis appeared to prove the cliché that offense wins games but defense wins titles.

Down 2-1 in the series, Curry recorded the ninth 30-plus scoring game of his playoff career in Game 4 with 33 points on May 9, 2015. Looking every bit like the MVP from the regular season, Curry pumped in 21 points in the first half as the Warriors took a 17-point halftime lead and coasted to the finish with a 101-84 win – Curry also finished with 8 rebounds, 5 assists, and 2 steals while making 50 percent of his field goals. With the series tied at 2 games apiece, the Warriors retreated home to the Oracle Arena and demolished the Grizzlies 98-78 in their best game of the series on May 13, 2015. Curry scored 18 points on 6 three-pointers while adding 7 boards and 6 steals in an all-around performance in which he broke Ray Allen's record for the fewest number of postseason games to make 100 three-pointers. Curry accomplished the feat in 28 games, or 7 games less than Allen. He also became only the 10th player in the last 30 years to score at least 18 points in a playoff game exclusively from three-pointers and the first player in NBA history to hit 6 three-pointers and have 6 steals in a playoff game.

Two nights later, on May 15, 2015, Curry delivered the dagger that ended Memphis' season in Game 6 when he hit a Hail Mary from beyond half court to end the third quarter. The Grizzlies were then making a run, cutting a 15-point second-quarter deficit down to just 1 point late in the third period. The Warriors were up 5 points when Curry snatched a loose ball in the closing seconds of the third quarter and threw the 62-foot bomb that swished the nets.

With the Grizzlies and their crowd stunned, Curry punctured the nets with one three-pointer after another in a scorching finish that saw him set a Warriors' team record with 8 three-pointers. Curry finished with 32 points, 10 assists, and 6 rebounds to send the Golden State Warriors to win, 108-95, sending the team to its first Conference Finals' appearance since 1976. On May 18, 2015, the second-seeded Houston Rockets completed a near impossible comeback from being 3-1 down in their second-round playoff series to stun the Los Angeles Clippers and advance to the Western Conference Finals.

The Western Conference Finals series started on May 19, 2015, when Curry took the lead for the team by making 13 of 22 field goals (six of 11 from behind the three-point line) for a total of 34 points with 6 rebounds, 5 assists, and 2 steals in a close 110-106 win at home in the Oracle Arena. Curry made the final 9 points for Golden State, including the last 2 free throws in the final seconds to give the Warriors the 4-point lead with just four seconds left. In Game 2 on May 21, 2015, Curry sank 13 of 21 from the field, including 5 of 11 from behind the three-point line, for 33 points with 6 assists, 3 rebounds, and 1 steal in a 99-98 win, despite a late push by James Harden and Dwight Howard during a 8-2 run in the final minute and a half. The third game of the series wasn't close at all: It was a 115-80 Golden State win on May 23, 2015, at the Toyota Center in Houston, Texas. In that victory, Curry made 12 of 19 field goals (7 of 9 from three-point range) with 9 of 10 free throws to finish with 40 points, 7 assists, 5 rebounds, 2 steals, and 1 block. While Houston avoided the sweep in Game 4 with a 128-115 decision thanks to Harden's 45 points, the Warriors clinched the Western Conference title with a 104-90 win on May 27, 2015, at home. Curry made just 33.3 percent from the field while scoring 26 points and collecting 8 rebounds, 6 assists, and 5 steals. Wining the Western title set up a very interesting NBA Finals matchup between the young and offensive-powered Warriors against the Eastern Conference favorites, the Cleveland Cavaliers.

Curry had a good start in his NBA Finals debut with 10 of 20 from the field for 26 points, 8 assists, 4 rebounds, and 2 steals on June 4, 2015, during a 108-100 win at home. But Cleveland evened the series by taking Game 2 on June 7, 2015, with a 95-93 win in Oakland. James finished with 39 points, 16 rebounds, and 11 assists, while Curry struggled despite 19 points, as he made just 2 of 15 (13.3 percent) from three-point range and 5 of 23 (21.7 percent) overall from the field. The Cavaliers then took a 2-1 lead with a 96-91 home win at Cleveland's Quicken Loans Arena on June 9, 2015. Curry did a little better with a 50 percent field goal conversion that included 7 of 13 from behind the three-point arc for 27 points, 6 assists, 6 rebounds, and 3 steals. But James also earned his second consecutive triple-double with 40 points, 12 rebounds, 8 assists, 4 steals, and 2 blocks.

Golden State tied the series in Game 4 on June 11, 2015, when four players scored in double figures for the 103-82 win. Curry finished with 22 points after shooting 47.1 percent while collecting 7 assists; teammate Andre Iguodala had 22 points of his own with 8 rebounds. James had a tougher night of shooting, as just 31.8 percent of his field goals were good; he had 20 points, 12 rebounds, and 8 assists. The lesser-known Timofey Mozgov led the Cavaliers with 28 points. Golden State returned home to Oakland and earned a 104-91 win on June 14, 2015, when Curry was 13 of 23 from the field (56.6 percent), including 7 of 13 from behind the three-point line (53.8 percent) for 37 total points to go with 7 rebounds, 4 assists, and 2 steals. That win gave the Warriors the lead entering Game 6. James was the lone bright spot for Cleveland with yet another playoff triple-double (40 points, 14 rebounds, and 11 assists) in another loss in the NBA Finals.

The Warriors made history by winning on June 16, 2015, by a score of 105-97 in Game 6 of the NBA Finals. Small runs added up to a 10-point lead in the middle of the fourth quarter before Golden State went on a three-point shooting spree between Curry, Iguodala, and Thompson helped give the Warriors a 92-77 lead with six minutes left in the game. Curry hit 5 of 6 free throws in the final minute to help maintain the lead against a Cavaliers team that began to intentionally foul the Warriors to buy time and possessions. Curry finished tied with Iguodala for the team lead with 25 points; he also had 8 assists, 6 rebounds, and 3 steals. The Golden State win came despite James having another amazing individual performance in a Cleveland loss – 32 points, 18 rebounds, and 9 assists.

It was a great ending to a season after Golden State went 67-15 on the season – which was a franchise record – and won their first NBA Championship since the 1975 season. While Iguodala won the NBA Finals Most Valuable Player Award, Curry still had the MVP honors for his regular-season efforts; he averaged 26 points, 6.3 assists, and 5.2 rebounds during the six-game series with Cleveland. But he had better overall numbers in the regular season with 23.8 points, 7.7 assists, 4.3 rebounds, and 2 steals per game while converting on 48.7 from the field (44.3 from behind the three-point arc). For those who watched Curry struggle with injuries in his first three seasons while Golden State missed the playoffs, it felt as if the organization's patience for their star athlete had paid off.

In a *Sports Illustrated* feature that ran after the NBA Finals, Curry said winning the championship felt more special after the difficulties with health and his ankles early in his career and being able to hold the championship trophy six years after starting his career in the NBA[xxi]. Now the only thing to do was prove it all over again; a challenge Curry and the rest of the Golden State Warriors were excited to take on as the defending NBA Champions.

2016 Season – Being the Best[xxii]

A few hours after their championship banner was raised in Oakland's Oracle Center[xxiii], the Golden State Warriors started a new season on October 27, 2015, with a 111-95 win over the New Orleans Pelicans. Curry made 14 of 26 from the field (53.8 percent), including 5 of 12 from three-point range (41.7 percent) to score 40 points in the first game of the NBA's 2015-16 season; he also collected 7 assists, 6 rebounds, and 2 steals. Curry and the rest of the Golden State Warriors were picking up right where they left off – winning games. Granted, it was slightly different with head Coach Steve Kerr taking a break after recovering from back surgery. The team's assistant Coach Luke Walton – son of basketball legend Bill Walton and veteran of 11 seasons in the NBA with the Los Angeles Lakers and the Cleveland Cavaliers – took over on an interim basis. With the stars that Golden State on the roster, Walton inherited quite a group to start his head coaching career in the NBA.

In fact, the Warriors won their first 24 games to start the regular season – a streak in which Curry averaged 32.5 points, 6.1 assists, 5.3 rebounds, and 2.1 steals. During that run, Curry's best individual game was easily on October 31, 2015, in a 134-120 win – ironic how Curry continued to be a nightmare for the New Orleans Pelicans on Halloween night. After shooting 63 percent from the field (17 of 27) featuring 57.1 percent from three-point range (8 of 14) and a perfect 11 for 11 on the foul line, Curry finished the game with 53 points, 9 assists, 4 rebounds, and 4 steals. The second-leading scorer for the Warriors was Draymond Green with 21 points. Curry had his first double-double of the NBA season on November 6, 2015, during a 119-104 win at home against the Denver Nuggets, in which Curry led the team, again, with 34 points and 10 assists; he also added 7 rebounds, 3 steals, and 1 block in the game. Curry was also close to hitting the 50-point mark on November 12, 2015, during a 129-116 win on the road against the Minnesota Timberwolves – he made 15 of 25 from the field (60 percent) and 61.5 percent from long distance to have 46 points, 5 rebounds, 4 assists, and 2 steals.

When a team starts the season on what seems to be a historic undefeated streak, the opposing teams bring their "A" games, each hoping to end the streak, which can sometimes give that team a little boost for their own season. As the Warriors continued to go through November without losing a game, the competition got a lot harder and there seemed to be pressure about when the streak was going to end. On November 30, 2015, the Warriors played the Utah Jazz in a very close road contest where Curry broke a 101-101 tie with a 26-foot field goal for 3 points in the final minute and sank 2 more free throws for security in the final seconds to give Golden State the 106-103 win. Curry led the team with 26 points, making just 45 percent from the field while collecting 6 rebounds, 5 assists, and 2 steals. After winning their 20th game of the season over the Charlotte Hornets on December 2, 2015, Golden State found themselves in another tough road contest against the Toronto Raptors on December 5, 2015. Curry and Thompson combined for a perfect 6 for 6 from the foul line to hold off Toronto for a 112-109 win. Curry kept the Warriors in the game with 44 points, converting on 58.3 percent of his total shots, including 9 of 15 from the three-point range; he also collected 7 assists and 2 rebounds.

Wins on the road against the Brooklyn Nets (114-98), the Indiana Pacers (131-123) and the Boston Celtics (124-119) increased the streak to 24 games[xxiv]. They had the longest winning streak to begin a season in league history and the third longest overall; the 1971-72 Los Angeles Lakers won 33 straight games, while the 2012-13 Miami Heat had a run of 27 games in the second half of their season. But, as with all good things, an end was inevitable. However, the team that defeated them might have been a surprise, as the Warriors lost on the road to the Milwaukee Bucks on December 12, 2015; the win elevated the Bucks to 10-15 at the time. While Curry made 45.5 percent from the field for 28 points, he was not effective from long range as he made just 2 out of 9 (22.2 percent) three-point attempts while collecting 7 rebounds and 5 assists.

So how does a team that loses their first game of the season in December respond against another below-.500 team in the Phoenix Suns? Earn a blowout victory by a score of 128-103 on December 16, 2015. The other Splash Brother, Klay Thompson, led the team with 43 points, making 15 of 22 from the field (68.2 percent), including 8 out of 13 from the three-point range (61.5 percent). Curry still had a good game, scoring 25 points; he made 10 of 14 from the field (71.4 percent) while collecting 7 assists. A few days later, on December 18, 2015, Golden State exacted some revenge against the Milwaukee Bucks with a 121-112 win at their home court in the Oracle Arena. Curry nearly had a triple-double with 26 points, 10 rebounds, and 9 assists while making 50 percent of his field goals and 10 of 11 from the foul line. A little more than a week later, Curry got another triple-double on December 28, 2015, with 23 points, 14 rebounds, and 10 assists, hitting 43.8 percent of his field goal attempts (6 of 13 from three-point range) to help the Warriors get the 122-103 win at home over the Sacramento Kings.

The Warriors suffered their second loss of the season on December 30, 2015, a 114-91 defeat on the road by the Dallas Mavericks in a game where Curry did not play because of an injury to his left shin suffered during the win over the Sacramento Kings. He also missed the game on December 31, 2015, but Golden State earned that road win, 114-110 over the Houston Rockets, thanks to Klay Thompson's 38 points and 7 rebounds. Curry made an attempt to fight through the pain by trying to make the start against the Denver Nuggets on January 2, 2016 at home, but he played just 14½ minutes. In that brief span, he made 2 of 6 field goals for 5 points, along with 4 assists and 2 steals in a close 111-108 overtime win. Curry played more, nearly 32 minutes, in a start against the Charlotte Hornets on January 4, 2016, for a 111-101 win. Curry went 12 of 21 from the field (5 of 10 from three-point range) to score 30 points to go along with 4 assists, 3 rebounds, and 2 steals. His Splash Brother teammate Thompson also scored 30 points by making 11 of 23 from the field (6 of 11 from three-point range) while collecting 5 rebounds, 3 assists, and 1 block. Curry continued to fight through the pain during the team's 109-88 win over the Los Angeles Lakers, in which he made 6 of 13 field goals (four of 8 from three-point land) for 17 points with 6 assists and 3 steals. However, *Sports Illustrated*'s Ben Golliver reported that Curry suffered another ding to his left shin that left him hobbling on the court in the middle of the third quarter, which is why he played only about 28 minutes of the game. He was obviously hurting before coming into the game, since he was wearing a pad against the Lakers on January 5, 2016. Curry reportedly told the media that the team's doctors informed him the shin would need about four weeks to fully heal; yet he intended to play through the pain regardless.

Curry had some struggles during those four weeks, as in the team's 128-108 win over the Portland Trail Blazers on January 8, 2016. In that game, he made just 8 of 18 from the field (44.4 percent) and only 4 of 11 from the three-point distance (36.4 percent) to score 26 points with 9 assists, 3 rebounds, and 1 steal. Then there were games where you wouldn't have noticed it when looking at his numbers. One of the best examples came on January 9, 2016, during a 128-116 win over the Sacramento Kings. Curry led the Warriors with 28 points, 11 assists, 6 rebounds, 1 steal, and 1 block while making 57.1 percent from the field (12 of 21) and an equal percentage from three-point range (8 of 14). Curry followed that up with another 31 points and 6 assists during the Warriors' 111-103 win over the Miami Heat.

Curry had another great game with 38 points, 9 assists, 5 rebounds, 3 steals, and 1 block while making 13 of 25 field goals (52 percent), but just 5 of 12 from three-point range (41.7 percent) in a 112-110 loss to the Denver Nuggets on January 13, 2016. It was only the third loss Golden State had suffered all season. The Warriors bounced back rather quickly with a 116-98 win at home over the Los Angeles Lakers on January 14, 2016. Curry made 9 of 18 from the field, with most of his shots taken from the three-point distance (8 of 16). He finished the game with 26 points, 6 rebounds, 3 assists, and another steal. The Warriors suffered another loss on January 16, 2016, by a score of 113-95 while visiting the Detroit Pistons. Curry had another high-scoring outing with 38 points, making 13 of 26 from the field overall and 7 of 15 from three-point range (46.7 percent). He also collected 7 rebounds, 5 assists, and 2 steals. But the Pistons had a big game with double digits by all five of their starters – 20 points each from Reggie Jackson and Kentavious Caldwell-Pope – and 12 points from Aron Baynes off the bench. Losing two out of three games, including one to the mediocre Detroit Pistons, caused some concerns about whether the Warriors would be able to maintain their effort to catch the 1995-96 Chicago Bulls.

However, Golden State went on another winning streak to conclude the first half of the NBA season before the 2016 NBA All-Star Game. It started on January 18, 2016, when the Warriors earned a blowout win on the road over the Cleveland Cavaliers, 132-98. Curry made 12 of 28 from the field (66.7 percent) and 7 of 12 from three-point range (58.3 percent) while making all 4 of his free throws for 35 total points to go along with 5 rebounds, 4 assists, and 3 steals. Curry then had a double-double with 25 points and 11 assists while collecting another 7 rebounds, 2 steals, and 1 block as Golden State defeated the Chicago Bulls on the road on January 20, 2016 – Curry made 8 of 18 from the field (44.4 percent) and a perfect 6 of 6 on the foul line. Two nights later, on January 22, 2016, Curry recorded his second triple-double of the season, when he made 8 of 15 from behind the three-point arc (53.3 percent) to allow him to score 39 points with 12 assists and 10 rebounds in the team's 40th win of the season over the Indiana Pacers, 122-110.

The streak continued on January 25, 2016 against the team with the second-best record in the Western Conference, the San Antonio Spurs. This game was considered by many a possible look at the Western Conference Finals when the playoffs roll through in the month of May. The Warriors' defense held the Spurs to just 41.9 percent from the field, with the team led by Kawhi Leonard's 16 points while the others struggled. On the other side, Curry made 12 of 20 from the field (60 percent), including 6 of nine from behind the three-point arc (66.7 percent), and converted 7 of 7 from the foul line to score 37 points; he also had 5 steals.

But the big part of a team's success isn't just one player being the leading scorer in all 82 games of the regular season. The Golden State Warriors can find their offense from other players in games when Curry isn't at his best. For example, when Golden State hosted the Dallas Mavericks on January 27, 2016, Curry made just 4 of 11 from the field (36.4 percent), with 3 of 7 from three-point range (42.9 percent) for just 14 points, while collecting 9 assists, 3 steals, 2 rebounds, and 1 block. Klay Thompson led the team with 45 points, making 14 of 20 from the field (70 percent), including 7 of 12 from behind the three-point line (58.3 percent), and all 10 free throws to go along with 5 rebounds, 2 blocks, and 1 steal as the Warriors defeated the Mavericks 127-107.

Also, Curry wasn't responsible for all of the game-winning shots. On January 30, 2016, during a road game against the Philadelphia 76ers – who were just 7-40 going into the contest – the game was tied at 105-105 before Draymond Green passed to the open Harrison Barnes for a 23-foot basket with one second left that gave Golden State a 108-105 win. Curry still had an efficient game, making 9 of 19 from the field (47.4 percent) for 23 points, 6 assists, 5 rebounds, 2 blocks, and 1 steal in a little more than 34 minutes. Curry had one of his worst shooting performances with just 29.4

percent from the field for only 13 points during a 116-95 win on the road against the New York Knicks on January 31, 2016; but Thompson led the Warriors with 34 points while Green had a triple-double with 20 points, 10 rebounds, and 10 assists – the first of many for Green.

Then again, Curry is a reigning NBA MVP for a reason, as he showed on February 3, 2016, during another road win against the Washington Wizards, 134-121. He made 19 of 28 from the field (67.9 percent) and was most effective from behind the three-point arc by sinking 11 of 15 (73.3 percent) for a total of 51 points. He also had 7 rebounds, 3 steals, and 2 assists while Green had another triple-double with 12 points, 12 assists, and 10 rebounds. Curry followed that up with a double-double of his own with 26 points and 10 assists to go along with 6 rebounds and 3 steals in a 116-108 win over Oklahoma City Thunder on February 6, 2016; Curry could have had more points, but only made 10 of 26 from the field (38.5 percent) and only 1 of 9 from three-point range.

In the final games before the All-Star break, Curry continued to prove that he is one of the league's best players by making 7 of 16 from three-point distance and 12 of 24 overall for 34 points, 9 assists, 5 rebounds, and 1 steal during Golden State's 123-110 win at home over the Houston Rockets on February 9, 2016. One night later, on the road against the Phoenix Suns on February 10, 2016, Curry played only 30 minutes and made 9 of 17 from the field

(52.9 percent) and half of his attempts from three-point distance for 26 points while collecting 9 rebounds and 9 assists to help the Warriors get the 112-104 win. His teammate Thompson had 24 points of his own, so the Splash Brothers combined for 50 points.

The win over the Phoenix Suns elevated the Golden State Warriors to a record of 48-4 to lead the entire NBA with the best record and put them ahead of schedule in their efforts to surpass the 72 wins that the 1995-96 Chicago Bulls amassed to set the record for victories in a single season. Curry has missed only two games as of this writing and has averaged 29.8 points, 6.6 rebounds, 5.3 rebounds, and 2.1 steals in what could easily be another MVP quality season; he's also converted 50.8 percent of his field goal attempts (45.4 percent from three-point range). He's currently on pace to have the best season of his career – his highest scoring average came in the 2013-14 season, when he scored 24 points per game. In his MVP season, Curry averaged a little under that, with 23.8 points per game.

2016 NBA All-Star Weekend

Curry was voted into his third consecutive All-Star Game, to be played February 14, 2016, in Toronto, Canada. But, while Curry and Golden State teammates Klay Thompson and Draymond Green were named to the team, this was a year where a lot of attention went to Kobe Bryant, a veteran who was in the middle of his 20th and final season in the NBA[xxv]. This was his 18th All-Star Game appearance and part of his farewell tour in professional basketball. Both Bryant and Curry were selected as members of the Western Conference's starting 5 for the game, along with Oklahoma City Thunder's Kevin Durant and Russell Westbrook, as well as the San Antonio Spurs' Kawhi Leonard. It was a decent lineup with reserves that included Houston's James Harden, New Orleans' Anthony Davis and Sacramento's DeMarcus Cousins to face the Eastern Conference's LeBron James (Cleveland), Paul George (Indiana), Dewayne Wade (Miami) and other players from across the eastern half of North America.

On the day before the All-Star Game, Curry competed in the Foot Locker three-point contest held at the Air Canada Centre in Toronto, Canada. The rest of the field featured Houston Rockets' James Harden, Golden State teammate Klay Thompson, and Miami Heat veteran Chris Bosh[xxvi]. Curry entered the competition as the defending champion with 27 points out of 30 from the championship round in 2015, which really shouldn't surprise anyone who follows Curry's shooting habits with any regularity. This year's three-point contest was different, with the first four racks having four regular basketballs worth 1 point each and a money ball worth 2 points. The fifth and final rack was all money balls, so the possible highest point total was 34.

Curry did well in the first round with 21 points out of the possible 30, but he also cheered on his Golden State teammate Thompson, who had 22 points. They finished above the three players tied for the third place who had to compete in a tiebreaker round; they were Houston's James Harden, Phoenix's Devin Booker, and J.J. Redick of the Los Angeles Clippers, each of whom had 20 points in the first round. Toronto's Kyle Lowry had just 15 points, while Portland's C.J. McCollum had 14 points. There was a tiebreaker held to decide who would join defending champion Curry and Thompson in the final round. Booker won a 30-second tiebreaker contest with 10 points, edging out Redick's 9 points and Harden's 8 points to advance the final three.

Booker started the championship final round with 12 points, followed by the defending champion Curry going in and having a decent round with a score of 21 points. Then came Thompson, who had a few bounce off the rim before the final rack, where Thompson hit all of his shots to finish with a score of 27 points for a little bit of NBA history for the Splash Brothers. Curry and Thompson were the first teammates to win consecutive three-point contests. If both return in the 2017 NBA All-Star Weekend, who's to say that one of the two can't make it a third year for the Golden State Warriors?

On February 14, 2016, Curry and the Western Conference All-Stars participated in a very high-scoring All-Star Game in which they defeated the East, 196-173, at the Air Canada Centre. Curry played almost 29 minutes and made 10 of 18 from the field, highlighted by 6 of 13 from behind the three-point line for a total of 26 points to go along with 6 assists, 5 rebounds, and 4 steals. Curry's Golden State teammates both had decent games as well: Thompson had 9 points, 2 rebounds, 2 assists, and 1 steal, while Green had 4 points, 5 rebounds, and 2 steals. In his final All-Star Game, Bryant scored just 10 points with 7 assists and 6 rebounds after making only 4 of 11 from the field; it was a privilege for Curry to be a part of a future Hall of Famer's last All-Star moment.

After having such an impressive run in the 2016 All-Star Game, there are a lot of expectations for the remainder of the 2016 regular season and potentially another championship run for Golden State. We'll just have to see how the finals months conclude.

Looking Ahead in 2016

The Golden State Warriors are by far the best team in the NBA and it's looking more like they are chasing history in an attempt to surpass those 72 wins by the 1995-96 Chicago Bulls. The comparison between Michael Jordan then and Stephen Curry now has begun and the numbers that they each put up entering the NBA All-Star break are very similar. During the All-Star break in 1996, Jordan's Bulls were 42-5 while he scored an average of 30.8 points per game while converting on 50 percent of his field goals. But

Jordan was averaging about 38 minutes per game and Curry's minutes per game are down to about 33.8, mostly because he hasn't seen much action in the fourth quarter this season. Still, 20 years after Jordan, Curry's Warriors entered the break with a record of 48-4 while he averaged about 29.8 points and made 51 percent of his field goal attempts. Keep in mind that the Jordan in the 1995-96 NBA season later won the MVP awards in the regular season and during the NBA Finals which the Bulls won.

But Curry just wants to win and, with one of the best starts any NBA team has ever had, his Warriors hope to continue the momentum they've developed so far. Curry stated in an interview with CNN.com that he and the rest of the Golden State team want to break the 72-win season record set by Chicago years ago; there's no hiding it. Curry said that's because there aren't a lot of teams who have a chance to come close to the record during the season – even though the main goal in the end for Golden State is to return to the NBA Finals this June and win the league championship.

"But when you have a shot at history and being the best regular-season team in the history of the NBA, I think you've got to go for it," Curry said during the CNN.com interview with Jill Martin on February 12, 2016. Regardless whether the team gets to the magical 73-win number, it should be quite an interesting second half of the 2015-16 season.

Chapter 5: International Competition

While most basketball players dream of being a star in the NBA, there is always something special about wearing the red, white, and blue like the members of the Dream Team from the 1990s who won gold at the Olympic Games. With the popularity of basketball growing around the world, being a part of international competition does improve a player's stock in many ways, such as showing how valuable they are to the NBA and their teams. Endorsements are also commonplace for those who join Team USA on the basketball court. It should be no surprise to any basketball fan that Curry has played in international tournaments.

In addition to all of the accolades that Curry has accumulated in his time both at Davidson College and with the Golden State Warriors, he helped win a few gold medals during competitions under the International Basketball Federation (FIBA). Being a part of Team USA is something that many great players in the NBA are honored to do and they consider themselves to be among the selected few to wear the same uniform that basketball legends like Michael Jordan and Grant Hill have worn in the past. To say the least, the expectations are high for any USA team competing internationally and Curry would help meet some of those goals overseas.

2010 FIBA World Cup in Turkey[xxvii]

This tournament began with the preliminary round of group play, and the United States was in Group B, with all of the games played in Istanbul. Their first game ended in success on August 28, 2010, with a 106-78 win over Croatia; Eric Gordon of the Los Angeles Clippers led the team with 16 points. Curry was not very effective, with just 2 of 6 field goals and he missed all 3 attempts from behind the three-point line for just a total of 4 points. The U.S. team followed that up the next day with a 99-77 win over Slovenia, in which Curry had only 3 points on his lone attempt from long distance. Curry did not play in America's close 70-68 win over Brazil on August 30, 2010, when Durant led the team with 27 points.

Curry scored 4 points after making 2 of 5 from the field in just 17 minutes to go with 5 assists, 4 rebounds, and 1 steal to help Team USA defeat Iran, 88-51, on September 1, 2010. While his numbers were limited in the few minutes he played during the first few games, he had much better luck in the 92-57 win over Tunisia on September 2, 2010, when he converted 5 out of 8 field goals, including 3 of 5 from behind the three-point line, to finish with 13 points. Curry also collected 3 rebounds and 2 assists in that game. The win gave the United States a perfect 5-0 record to win Group B and advance to the knockout stage.

On September 6, 2010, USA earned a very decisive blowout victory over Angola, 121-66, in the first round; four American players scored in double figures (led by 19 points from Chauncey Billups and 17 from Rudy Gay, Gordon, and Durant). Curry had only 5 points, after making 2 of 6 field goals (1 of 5 from three-point range) to go along with 3 assists and 2 steals. Curry followed that up with just 2 points from free throws in the team's 89-79 win over Russia on September 9, 2010, in the quarterfinals of the tournament; he played only five minutes. Curry also only scored 3 points on his lone field goal during a brief two minutes in the semifinals win over Lithuania, 89-74, on September 11, 2010. Curry repeated that field goal in the finals victory over Turkey, 81-64, on September 12, 2010. Durant won the tournament's Most Valuable Player award after he scored 28 points after shooting 58.8 percent from the field to help the United States have a perfect 9-0 record and the gold medal.

It was a quality team that won the FIBA World Cup for the first time since 1994. Granted, this team that competed in the 2010 FIBA World Cup was considered a "B team," since many of the players who were invited did not participate for a number of reasons – injury, needing rest, focusing on free agency in the NBA, and other personal commitments. While Curry didn't have the impact on Team USA like some of the earlier mentioned basketball legends, he was still part of an all-star team and there were a number of other talented players who averaged less than 10 minutes per game, including Danny Granger, Kevin Love, and Tyson Chandler. Because of how well the team did during the tournament, many members of Team USA's executive staff noted they would be willing to considering bringing these players back for future tryouts for future tournaments, including Curry.

2014 FIBA World Cup in Spain[xxviii]

After having continued success in the 2012 Summer Olympics held in London, England, the United States was hoping to add more gold to their trophy case at the 2014 FIBA World Cup held in Barcelona, Spain. The U.S. automatically qualified for the tournament after winning in 2010 and the American team featured a combination of players from the 2010 FIBA World Cup team, the 2012 Olympics team, and additional players from across the NBA under head Coach Mike Krzyzewski, the iconic coach known for his time at Duke University.

Curry started the game against Finland on August 30, 2014, but wasn't very effective, going only 1 of 6 from the field and missing all 5 shots from behind the three-point arc for 4 points. But he led Team USA with 5 assists to help earn the 114-55 win. Klay Thompson led the team with 18 points while Anthony Davis scored 17. Curry followed that up by making 3 of 6 from three-point range to finish with 9 points, 5 steals, 3 assists, and 2 rebounds to help the United States earn a 98-77 win on August 31, 2014. After a day of rest, Team USA defeated New Zealand, 98-71, on September 2, 2014. Curry had another productive game with 12 points, making 4 of 7 from the field (2 of 4 from three-point range) to go along with 5 rebounds, 3 assists, 2 steals, and 1 blocked shot.

During the preliminary Group C play, Curry had 8 points, 7 assists, and 6 rebounds, converting 42.9 percent of his field goals, to help the United States earn a 106-71 victory on September 3, 2014. He followed that with a much better offensive performance, making 3 of 6 field goal attempts (3 of 4 from three-point distance) and a perfect 5 for 5 from the foul line for a total of 14 points to go with 1 assist, 1 rebound, and 1 steal in a 95-71 win over Ukraine on September 4, 2014. Once again, the U.S. finished the preliminary round with a perfect 5-0 record to advance to the knockout stage where a loss would send them home.

Curry had his best international game ever on September 6, 2014, during an 86-63 win over Mexico. He shot 70 percent from the field, doing most of his damage from behind the three-point line by making 6 of 9 from that range for a total of 20 points. He also added 4 assists, tying Chicago Bulls' star Derrick Rose for the team lead, 3 rebounds, and 1 steal. Curry couldn't continue the offensive momentum as he only made 2 of 9 from the field for 6 points during a 119-76 win over Slovenia in the quarterfinals of the FIBA tournament. Team USA again faced Lithuania in the FIBA

World Cup semifinals on September 11, 2014, and earned the same result with a 96-68 win. Curry bounced back with 4 of 8 from the field (3 of 6 from three-point range) to score 13 points, with 3 rebounds and 1 assist, while the Cleveland Cavaliers' Kyrie Irving led the team with 18 points.

Team USA recaptured the gold medal on September 14, 2014, with a 129-92 win over Serbia. Irving led the team with 26 points and Curry added 10 points, making 2 of 7 three-point field goals and all 4 free throw attempts. It was another dominant performance by the entire team, with the average margin of victory about 33 points per game. The win over Serbia in the FIBA tournament finals gave Curry and the other NBA stars gold medals and also an automatic berth for the United States to compete in the 2016 Summer Olympics in Rio de Janeiro, Brazil.

Will Curry Play in 2016 Olympics?

On August 6, 2015, Curry was one of the 34 players from 21 different NBA teams who were named to the initial men's national team minicamp that was held at Las Vegas, Nevada[xxix]. The list also featured other NBA stars such as LeBron James (Cleveland Cavaliers), Kevin Durant (Oklahoma City Thunder) and Klay Thompson (Golden State Warriors). Curry was considered one of the standout players from the recent 2014 FIBA World Cup team that the USA Basketball program wanted to bring back in an effort to have a stronger team for the upcoming 2016 Olympics in Rio de Janeiro, Brazil. Other players from the 2014 World Cup team who joined Curry at the initial minicamp included his teammate Thompson, Kyrie Irving, and James Harden; as well as past Olympians James, Durant, and Kevin Love.

As the current 2015-2016 season progressed, there were evaluations and discussions among the coaching staff led by head Coach Mike Krzyzewski (Duke University) and assistants Jim Boeheim (Syracuse University), Tom Thibodeau (formerly of the Chicago Bulls), and Monty Williams (Oklahoma City Thunder). On January 18, 2016, the list of the 30 finalists was released by USA Basketball; Curry was among the names and given the No. 43 jersey. A few of his teammates also made the finalist list – forward Harrison Barnes, forward Draymond Green, guard/forward Andre Iguodala and guard Klay Thompson.

The chairman of USA Basketball, Jerry Colangelo, stated that the depth of the 2016 team was extraordinary when compared to past years preparing for the Olympics. It was tough to trim down to the 30 names and now the group has to cut down to 12 players for the Olympics. There are plenty of basketball fans and some experts who believe Curry should be a shoo-in because of his threat from the three-point range. While he hasn't shown it in all of his past international experiences, he has improved greatly as one of the most dangerous scoring threats in the NBA for arguably the best team in the league the past couple of season. It's very likely that the coaches and chairman have looked at how Curry is currently performing in his team's pursuit to have the best record in NBA history.

The 2016 Olympic Games will take place Aug. 5-21; 12 countries will compete in the men's basketball tournament. Expectations are always high for the USA, since they have an all-time record of 130 wins and 5 losses in Olympic competition with a total of 14 gold medals, a silver, and two bronze; they have never left an Olympics without some kind of hardware. With the talent available to the program now, including players like Curry, LeBron, and Irving, it's hard to imagine the United States leaving Brazil with anything less than a gold medal.

Chapter 6: Curry's Personal Life

It is a well-known fact that Steph is one of three children of former NBA sharpshooter Dell Curry. Not everybody knows that his mother Sonya played volleyball at Virginia Tech, and was considered the team's star at that time. His siblings are involved with sports as well. His brother Seth was part of Duke University's basketball squad for three seasons and his sister Sydel Curry plays volleyball at Elon University. The Curry family developed tight bonds over the years and the fact that Dell Curry resigned as a coach for the Charlotte Bobcats before the start of the 2007 NBA season so that he could watch his son's college games is proof of that commitment. Dell has also praised his son, saying that he is very proud to have watched Steph grow up and play the game that he played and that his son is even better than he was.

Steph Curry grew up with devout Christian parents in a household where a morning family devotional time was a must. Curry stated in an interview that he gave himself to Christ in the fourth grade at the Central Church of God in Charlotte. His parents continued to support his faith and made sure that he fully understood his commitment. He is now one of the best young players in the NBA and a leader of a playoff squad, but he is also a devoted husband and father as well. An interesting fact about Curry is that he always writes biblical verses on his shoes. Some of his favorites include

Philippians 4:13 and Romans 8:28 (which is also his mother's favorite).

On July 30, 2011, Steph married his high school sweetheart, Ayesha Alexander, whom he had met in a church youth group when he was 15. After finishing high school, Ayesha decided to pursue her acting career in Los Angeles where she had roles in the "Whittaker Bay" and "Hannah Montana" television series. Steph went to a basketball camp on the West Coast and contacted her through Facebook for the first time after high school, and the rest is history. The couple has two daughters: Riley, born in 2011, and Ryan, born in 2015. On the day of their wedding, the couple asked all guests that they donate funds to the Thanks USA organization instead of bringing wedding gifts. The organization supports families of United States military personnel.

Steph's younger brother Seth accomplished one feat that Steph did not manage to do; he played for the Duke Blue Devils, regarded as having one of the best college basketball programs in the country. Seth was part of Duke's program while in college for three full seasons after he transferred from a small program at Liberty University. Even though he averaged 17.5 points on 46.5% shooting, Seth went undrafted in 2013 and has failed to make an NBA roster since then. An injury suffered during his last season at Duke really hurt Seth's draft stock. He played a preseason game for the Golden State Warriors and he spent 30 seconds on the floor together with his brother. Since then he has remained a D-League standout averaging 19.5 games and was a part of this year's D-League All-Star team, bidding his time until an NBA franchise takes notice. Seth had a short stint with the Orlando Magic this preseason, and currently plies his trade with their D-League affiliate, the Erie Bayhawks.

An interesting fact about Steph is that he also loves to play golf. Steph considers it to be his second sport. At one point there was even a news article that explored why he did not want to play in Minnesota, and one of the main reasons was the bad golf weather out there. He later laughed that off as an inaccurate statement and said that he can always find the time and place for a good game of golf.

Steph's mother taught him the importance of finishing his education while he was young. During the NBA lockout in 2011, while his colleagues were busy touring, finding overseas jobs or fancy internships, Steph went back to college at Davidson. He enrolled in courses with the objective of finishing his sociology degree. He reunited with Coach McKillop and practiced with the basketball team whenever he could, offering them input from a unique perspective. He even worked on a senior research project about NBA players' tattoos as it relates to their public image, tabbing former teammates Monta Ellis and Anthony Morrow as his primary sources.

Chapter 7: Impact on Basketball

Since he entered Davidson College at the age of 18 until now, Curry has affected numerous lives, organizations, and associations while changing the game of basketball as a whole. The biggest reason for his success is because he is a dedicated individual with clearly defined goals, which has been proven many times throughout his professional career and noticed in his personal life.

Curry shook things up when he reached the NCAA Elite 8 in 2008 and his team eliminated some higher-seeded teams, including Georgetown, Gonzaga, and Wisconsin. That impacted not only Davidson College, but also the whole college basketball world in general. Curry proved that even smaller Division I schools can build a great team, improve their organization in the span of a year, and produce one of the biggest prospects in the NBA draft talent pool. He also proved wrong all of the major NCAA programs that rejected him because of his size. His play made a big statement to the world. Because of Curry, college organizations and NBA scouts nowadays give more and more credit to basketball IQ, shooting technique, command of the floor, and many other intangibles previously overlooked. It is easy to see that Curry has impacted the way young prospects are seen in the eyes of coaching staffs. As a result, it will probably be difficult to be selected as the number one draft pick in the near future solely based on vertical jump, wingspan, strength, and other purely physical attributes.

What Steph Curry did in his three years with the Wildcats was incredible. He faced a huge test when initially entering the NBA, having to answer the question of whether or not he could transfer his talents to the NBA level. There were many skeptics among basketball experts and general managers before the 2009 draft. The skepticism was probably why Curry ended up as the seventh overall pick for the Golden State Warriors behind players like Hasheem Thabeet and Jonny Flynn, who are now both out of the league. Now in his fifth NBA season, Curry has transformed the Warriors squad from a perennial lottery-bound team into a legitimate title contender. They have made the playoffs in consecutive seasons, a feat that has been accomplished only once in the past thirty-seven seasons of the franchise (1990-91 and 1991-1992). That was their famed "Run TMC" era, when they had former all-stars Tim Hardaway, Mitch Richmond, and Chris Mullin and they were coached by the much-accomplished Don Nelson.

Curry has managed to accomplish all of this due to his impeccable work ethic and positive attitude toward life. His crazy workout sessions get noticed today, but he has been known to practice hard since his high school days. He was once an attendee at a Kobe Bryant camp. According to one coach, Curry would start training each day one hour before anybody else was out there on the court. He had already made over a hundred shots before the actual practice began and would always try to make at least five free throws in a row after the practice finished. No matter how big or small the game, his family was there for him and taught him how to be a good person and achieve his goals through the help of Christianity.

All of this led Curry to become not only a great player and dedicated father, but a respected member of the community as well. He goes out of his way to help as much as he can and one proof of that is the story about his wedding gifts. Curry does not just show his unselfishness in NBA games or by signing an undervalued contract worth $44 million, but throughout his life as a whole.

On October 1, 2013 Curry signed a five-year shoe contract deal with fledgling apparel brand Under Armour, making him their main endorser. That was a big step for him because he had worn Nikes all of his life and he represented the brand during his first four years in the NBA. It speaks volumes about Curry's marketability that a brand on the rise like Under Armour wanted him to be their top ambassador. Under Armour also has on their roster guards like Brandon Jennings of the Detroit Pistons, Kemba Walker of the Charlotte Hornets, and Greivis Vasquez of the Toronto Raptors. Curry explained that the biggest factor in his decision to switch shoes was that he was very comfortable during his meeting with Under Armour representatives. Also, since they have fewer athletes to cater to, more people can be assigned to work with him in customizing his shoes, which is very important to him due to his history of ankle injuries. Another deciding factor was the way that the brand intended to market him, as an underdog. He said via an interview with *Complex Sneakers*, "Under Armour always talks about that underdog mindset that follows them in the basketball world and that's how I've been my whole career."

Under Armour announced last October through its CEO, Kevin Plank, that Curry will be getting his first signature shoe in 2015. According to reports, it will be called the UA Curry I. The brand also made a run at prying Kevin Durant away from Nike to pair with Curry this summer with an audacious 10-year $285 million offer, but Nike exercised their right to match it and Durant stayed put as a result.

Curry has made a substantial impact on his community's everyday life. He has changed the way prospects are perceived, taken the name of his beloved Davidson College to the highest level, and completely transformed a dying Warriors franchise. Steph Curry has created a public picture of himself as a true role model for young NBA fans. The truly amazing thing is that he managed to do all of this at the young age of 25 while remaining a dedicated family man and a true member of a local Christian community.

Chapter 8: Stephen Curry's Legacy and Future

Steph Curry transformed Davidson College. Davidson Wildcats Coach McKillop said that it is rare to find a player who not only leaves an imprint on a program but also puts all of his energy into developing his team's spirit. Curry returned the compliment as he said that McKillop helped him achieve his goals by explaining his (McKillop's) vision for Curry's career and, that being of similar faith, his coach always kept him grounded. He added that McKillop was a great leader. Curry's three seasons at Davidson will be remembered for many generations to come. He is one of only six players in Davidson history who made it to the NBA and the first after Brandon Williams, who played for the Warriors in the 1997-98 NBA season. His basketball exploits aren't the only reason that Curry is still beloved at Davidson. Many teammates, schoolmates, and team staff members gush about his positive attitude and friendliness toward everyone. They all claim that his fame hasn't changed who he is as a person, that he is still very humble and approachable, as he was in college. Lauren Biggers, a college friend, said that most Davidson alumni wanted to be identified with him. "Stephen is kind of a way for the rest of the world to learn that," she adds. "So I think alumni are really attached to him in that way. Now you can say, 'Oh, you know

Stephen Curry? That's my guy, that's my school.' I went to North Carolina, but I would never be like 'Yeah, Michael Jordan is my guy.'"

Even though he had NBA genes, Steph Curry did not enter college basketball as a top prospect. He developed into a scoring machine at Davidson and, as much as he received from the school, he also gave back a lot. After being rejected by a couple of NCAA division teams, including Duke, Curry decided to enter Davidson. It is interesting that just a couple of years later, after his second year in the NBA, Curry was selected for the United States national team led by Duke's Coach K.

Curry developed a close bond with Coach McKillop and his teammates at Davidson. He averaged 25.3 points for the team in three seasons and led the team to the Elite 8 tournament in 2008. In that year, the Wildcats had a 20-0 division record and earned the 10th seed in the NCAA Tournament.

The first game was played against Gonzaga. The team was losing by as many as eleven points at the start of the second half, but Curry put on a heroic display, scoring 30 points in the second half. This gave the Wildcats their first win in an NCAA Tournament since 1969. Something similar happened in the second round as well. Curry was limited to 5 points in the first half against heavy favorites Georgetown and his team was trailing by 17 points at one point. Curry scored 25 points in the second half, helping his team advance to the next round. Georgetown was the second-seeded team in the nation that year. The whole nation noticed Curry's talent as the Wildcats lost to the top-seeded Kansas Jayhawks after winning another battle versus third-seeded Wisconsin. Curry broke several records in the process, including most three-pointers in a season and he joined an elite group of players who scored more than 30 points in their first four games in the NCAA Tournament.

Stephen Curry made sure that Davidson's name would not be forgotten in the near future with his performances over his three years there. Now he has transferred his work ethic, attitude toward the game, and personal values into his NBA career. He has stated in an interview that he felt that God wanted to use him in the league to show that not all successful athletes live the celebrity lifestyle that comes with all the money and fame. He is a very dedicated and loving husband to his wife Ayesha and father to their daughters Riley and Ryan and he has avoided any problems with the law. The future looks bright for Steph Curry at the age of 25 as he has already left a significant legacy at Davidson College and in the NBA as well. The holder of the record for total three-pointers made in a regular season in the NBA and in the NCAA has a very optimistic future ahead of him. Steph Curry is emerging as one of the greatest point guards of the modern era. Some pundits have even pronounced him as the best shooter of all time, ranking him above shooting legends Ray Allen (who holds the NBA record for three-point shots made) and Reggie Miller (whom Allen surpassed).

They claim that this is because of the degree of difficulty of his shots. Because he is the team's primary ball handler most of the time, Curry has to create his own shots through a maze of dribble moves such as the crossover and hesitation dribble, as opposed to just catching it in rhythm and shooting, as most long-range shooters have the luxury of doing. LeBron even gave him a compliment, saying that it made Mario Chalmers dizzy when Curry gave him three "hesi's" (hesitation dribbles) before shooting over him. Steph is also the active leader in career three-point percentage with a 44.0 percent clip and is second all-time to his current coach, Steve Kerr.

It will be exciting to see he will go down in the record books years from now how. Curry has also proven that he is more than just a deadly shooter and scorer. In the eyes of many coaches and fellow players, he is one of the most complete point guards in the league. He showed in Mark Jackson's system that he can also facilitate for his team while scoring in bunches and now, in new Coach Kerr's system, he is as effective off the ball as he is with the ball in his hands. This, aside from his shooting, which made him famous, is a testament to his versatility and his willingness to expand his game. Most basketball junkies eagerly select Curry as one of the top three picks in fantasy drafts because of the well-roundedness of his stat line.

Curry's underdog story has also led to comparisons between him and another famous small player, Allen Iverson. The similarities probably end with their stature and scoring ability, as both have had very different paths to their careers. Curry was raised with loving parents by his side while the mercurial "AI" had a very difficult upbringing with a single mother and a non-existent father.

Curry's college Coach McKillop summarizes it best when asked about Steph's future. "Steph has a future in whatever endeavor he decides to pursue," he offered. "If Steph wanted to run for the mayor of Charlotte or the governor of the state, if Steph wanted to be a coach, if Steph wanted to be an entrepreneur, Steph Curry will accomplish it."

How about going down as the greatest shooter in the history of the game? Only time will tell. But if there is one thing for certain, it is that Curry has become a lot stronger over his years in the NBA. It wasn't long ago that he regularly had issues with keeping his ankles healthy in 2011 and 2012. According to a recent article from ESPN titled "How Stephen Curry got the best worst ankles in sports," Curry had some doubts when he was a patient for a world-famous orthopedic surgeon at the Southern California Orthopedic Institute in 2012 after having already had two ligaments reconstructed and several rolled ankles. That history included five sprains in just his first 26 games of his NBA career in 2011, well before he became the nightmare for some of the NBA's elite players, such as LeBron James and Kobe Bryant.

In the months that followed, Curry wasn't sure if he was ever going to play in the NBA again. But the ESPN feature by Pablo S. Torre talked about how he was demonstrating the work ethic that many of his coaches found back at the high school and collegiate level. So after he made some adjustments to how he jumps and moves around the court, Curry was able to show his true potential. At this writing, Curry and the Warriors are entering the 2016 NBA All-Star break with a record of 48-4, and many believe they will finish with at least 73 wins and becoming the lone team in history to finish with fewer than 10 losses – an achievement that was considered nowhere close to being possible. The only team close to them is San Antonio at 45-8. If this was any other season in NBA, having 45 wins against only 8 losses would be the best in the league. But the Warriors have been on fire and fans can only hope to see the Western Conference Finals between the Spurs and Warriors for a chance to play for the NBA Finals championship.

The second half of the NBA season is up in the air and there's no denying that the Golden State Warriors are pretty much pacing themselves to be the team to beat in the NBA, again. It's only a matter of health and how much momentum the Warriors can sustain. At least we know Curry's ankles are stronger than ever, so there's little chance for the injury issues that plagued his season. One thing is certain, we're going to find Curry playing some fourth-quarter minutes in the playoffs, which he has rarely done so far in the regular season – likely to preserve him for the long run and a push toward a second consecutive NBA Championship.

Final Word/About the Author

I was born and raised in Norwalk, Connecticut. Growing up, I could often be found spending many nights watching basketball, soccer, and football matches with my father in the family living room. I love sports and everything that sports can embody. I believe that sports are one of most genuine forms of competition, heart, and determination. I write my works to learn more about influential athletes in the hopes that from my writing, you the reader can walk away inspired to put in an equal if not greater amount of hard work and perseverance to pursue your goals. If you enjoyed *Stephen Curry: The Incredible Story of One of Basketball's Sharpest Shooters,* please leave a review! Also, you can read more of my works on *Colin Kaepernick, Aaron Rodgers, Peyton Manning, Tom Brady, Russell Wilson, Michael Jordan, LeBron James, Kyrie Irving, Klay Thompson, Stephen Curry, Kevin Durant, Russell Westbrook, Anthony Davis, Chris Paul, Blake Griffin, Kobe Bryant, Joakim Noah, Scottie Pippen, Carmelo Anthony, Kevin Love, Grant Hill, Tracy McGrady, Vince Carter, Patrick Ewing, Karl Malone, Tony Parker, Allen Iverson, Hakeem Olajuwon, Reggie Miller, Michael Carter-Williams, John Wall, James Harden, Tim Duncan, Steve Nash, Pau Gasol, Marc Gasol, Jimmy Butler, Dirk Nowitzki, Draymond Green and Pete Maravich* in the Kindle Store. If you love basketball, check out my website at

<u>claytongeoffreys.com</u> to join my exclusive list where I let you know about my latest books and give you lots of goodies.

Like what you read? Please leave a review!

I write because I love sharing the stories of influential people like Stephen Curry with fantastic readers like you. My readers inspire me to write more so please do not hesitate to let me know what you thought by leaving a review! If you love books on life, basketball, or productivity, check out my website at claytongeoffreys.com to join my exclusive list where I let you know about my latest books. Aside from being the first to hear about my latest releases, you can also download a free copy of *33 Life Lessons: Success Principles, Career Advice & Habits of Successful People*. See you there!

Clayton

References

[i] Rosen, Rick. "Dell Curry, Steph's Dad: Fast Facts You Need to Know." *Heavy.com*. Heavy, Inc. 27 May 2015. Web.

[ii] "Dell Curry College Stats." *Sports-Reference.com*. Sports Reference, LLC. N.d. Web.

[iii] "Dell Curry NBA Stats." *Basketball-Reference.com*. Sports Reference, LLC. N.d. Web.

[iv] "Steph Curry's Beautiful Half Haitian Mother Sonya Steals the Spotlight." *L'UnionSuite.com*. L'Union Creative, LLC. 15 June 2015. Web.

[v] Grange, Michael. "Curry's path to NBA stardom forged in Toronto." *Sportsnet.ca*. Rogers Digital Media. 14 Feb. 2015.

[vi] Ballingall, Alex. "Stephen Curry's Grade 8 Season at Tiny Toronto School Remembered." *TheStar.com*. Toronto Star Newspapers. 26 Feb. 2015. Web.

[vii] "Stephen Curry #30." *Rivals.com College Database*. Yahoo. N.d. Web.

[viii] Collins, Cory. "Stephen Curry started small, but he's always been big-time." *SportingNews.com*. Sporting News. 27 April 2015. Web.

[ix] Game notes from various Articles and Game Recaps. *DavidsonWildcats.com*. Davidson College. N.d. Web.

[x] NBA Stats come from "Steph Curry NBA Stats." *Basketball-Reference.com*. Sports Reference, LLC. N.d. Web.

[xi] Howard-Cooper, Scott. "Clutch shooting in the finals leads Pierce to Three-Point win." *NBA.com*. National Basketball Association. 14 Feb. 2010. Web.

[xii] "Rookies break sophomore hex in Dallas." *ESPN.com*. ESPN. 13 Feb. 2010.

[xiii] NBA Stats come from "Steph Curry NBA Stats." *Basketball-Reference.com*. Sports Reference, LLC. N.d. Web.

[xiv] NBA stats come from "Steph Curry NBA Stats." *Basketball-Reference.com*. Sports Reference, LLC. N.d. Web.

[xv] NBA Stats come from "Steph Curry NBA Stats." *Basketball-Reference.com*. Sports Reference, LLC. N.d. Web.

[xvi] NBA Stats come from "Steph Curry NBA Stats." *Basketball-Reference.com*. Sports Reference, LLC. N.d. Web.

[xvii] NBA Stats come from "Steph Curry NBA Stats." *Basketball-Reference.com*. Sports Reference, LLC. N.d. Web.

[xviii] NBA Stats from "Steph Curry NBA Stats." *Basketball-Reference.com*. Sports Reference, LLC. N.d. Web.

[xix] NBA Stats from "Steph Curry NBA Stats." *Basketball-Reference.com*. Sports Reference, LLC. N.d. Web.

[xx] NBA Stats from "Steph Curry NBA Stats." *Basketball-Reference.com*. Sports Reference, LLC. N.d. Web.

[xxi] Golliver, Ben. "Stephen Curry, Warriors cap charmed title run with fitting finish in the Finals." *SI.com*. Sports Illustrated. 17 June 2015. Web.

[xxii] NBA Stats from "Steph Curry NBA Stats." *Basketball-Reference.com*. Sports Reference, LLC. N.d. Web.

xxiii Freeman, Eric. "Golden State Warriors receive 2015 title rings, raise 1st banner in 40 years." *Ball Don't Lie*. Yahoo Sports. 27 October 2015. Web.

xxiv Reuters. "Warriors' 24-Game Winning Streak Ends With Loss to Bucks." *HuffingtonPost.com*. Huffington Post. 13 December 2015. Web.

xxv "NBA All-Star Game 2016." *NBA.com*. National Basketball Association. 14 February 2016. Web.

xxvi "Thompson Takes Foot Locker Three-Point Contest." *NBA.com*. National Basketball Association. 14 February 2016. Web.

xxvii Statistics, box scores from "FIBA World Championship 2010: Turkey." *Turkey2010FIBA.com*. International Basketball Federation. N.d. Web.

xxviii Stats, box scores from "FIBA World Championship 2014: Spain." *FIBA.com/Spain2014*. International Basketball Federation. N.d. Web.

xxix "USA Basketball Announced 34 Player Roster for 2015 Men's National Team Minicamp." *USAB.com*. USA Basketball. 6 August 2015. Web.

31756691R00086

Made in the USA
San Bernardino, CA
18 March 2016